THE ADVOCACY OF THE GOSPEL

THE ADVOCACY
OF THE GOSPEL

BY
DONALD SOPER

ABINGDON PRESS
New York Nashville

Copyright © 1961 by Donald Soper

PREFACE

This book contains six lectures given at the Yale Divinity School, in Spring 1960, under the Lyman Beecher Trust, which requires that such lectures should treat some aspect of Christian advocacy. Previous lecturers have adorned many themes intimately or more remotely associated with preaching. I have attempted no general study of the homiletic art, and I have made no claim to any novel or revolutionary theory of preaching. The approach in these lectures has been experimental, the background (to use the blessed word) existential, and the title is, I hope, self-explanatory and not belied by what follows it.

These lectures were preached, not read from script. There has been a bare minimum of alteration in the belief that to polish the literary style might well be to impair its immediacy. They read as they were spoken, and no attempt has been made to bring the topical illustrations up to date—although those which were obviously of local interest only have been removed. I venture to hope that whatever else may be found, or missed, in these pages something of the zest, as well as the responsibility, of Christian advocacy may be communicated to the reader as they are genuinely felt by the author.

DONALD SOPER

CONTENTS

21581

CONTENTS

CHAPTER I

THE SITUATION OF THE HEARER

ANY consideration of preaching in the light of the contemporary situation must appropriately begin by seeking, from the standpoint of the hearer, what that situation is. There are many respects in which the situation has radically altered and still is changing. We are faced as preachers with a heterogeneity of hearers where once our audience was much more homogenous.

In his day John Wesley had considerable difficulty in appealing to his congregation and was beset with all sorts of problems. A meat chopper wielded by a butcher in Nottingham was the kind of hazard with which he had to deal. As far as I know, however, when he spoke in the open air or indoors, he was not confronted with Buddhist priests. He was not challenged by a Moslem Sufi. In that sense, there is a vast difference between the kind of hearers normally gathering to listen to preachers in this day and generation from the kind of congregation which was accustomed to listen to John Wesley. I remember not so long ago, in the open air, being confronted by a Buddhist priest and discovering quite early in the proceedings, and not surprisingly, that he knew considerably more about Buddhism than I did. While this is not a common occurrence, to be sure, it does give point to the contention that, when we preach today, we are preaching to people who are likely to contain within their numbers those who have specialized in worlds of which our fathers were simply ignorant. When dealing with the state of the hearer today we are not *necessarily* confronted with those who know more about the subject than we do. But if we venture outside the realm of pure theology, it is highly likely that at least one member of our congregation will be a specialist in the field in which we are nothing better than tyros.

On the other hand, there is a contrary process which also limits the kind of group which is prepared to listen to preachers today. There is the selective process whereby the conforming group which is in the habit of listening to preachers does not represent the entire community, but represents at best one or two social, cultural and class grades in that community. We now know how true it was to regard industrialism as the most lethal drug ever to loosen the ties, and almost to destroy the religious sense itself, of those who became its victims, or its exponents. Though it might be argued that groups within the general industrial complex are still listening to preachers, it is much truer to say that, in general, the industrialized society, at least from the artisan downwards (in economic terms) is almost entirely remote from the words and indifferent to the message of the evangelist.

This problem is further exacerbated by the mobility of human beings today and their dislike of staying in any one place for any length of time. The number of holidays has increased. Nor is it likely in general that when people are on holiday they will receive, or desire to receive, spiritual ministrations. This means that so often our ministry is confined to certain sections of the year, and is also confined to such people as are more or less themselves confined to one particular area. In addition, the disposition of a great many people to move much more frequently than heretofore imposes a strain, because it makes it necessary for the man who preaches to preach spasmodically, as far as his hearer is concerned. Now these are probably superficial areas in which the state of the hearer is regarded, but they are important. But there are other matters which are far more fundamental.

I

The state of the hearer is today mainly secular. The religious background alike for those who go to church and those who stay away from church is largely destroyed. The two regulative factors in the religious background of our fathers was Sunday observance, very largely among those who belonged to the Protestant persuasion, and the Christian year as professed and observed much more largely by the Catholic groups. It is unquestionable that, though there is a disposition today on the part of people in this country and elsewhere to visit churches early on Sunday morning, their attendance is often based on the assumption that they will be required to do nothing more about it for the rest of Sunday. It is also dubious whether they will do anything more about it for the rest of the week.

This is not merely a passing phase. This breakdown of Sunday is a fundamental issue, and constitutes an element in the state of the hearer which is regulative and possessed of great potency either for good or ill. When I was a boy (if you'll pardon the reminiscence), the liturgy of Sunday was not confined to the services. Sunday was a liturgical occasion itself. The whole of Sunday for us, in a somewhat Roman and patriarchal and, if you like, narrow-minded household, was given over to a form of ecclesiastical liturgy. We began early in the morning with Sunday School. We then repaired to church. After church we came home to lunch, or to dinner as we then called it, and went back to Sunday School in the afternoon. After Sunday School in the afternoon, we went into the drawing-room for tea. My mother sat at the piano and we sang hymns until it was time to go back to church. We went to church and after church we came home, ate a large supper, and my father said it was a good thing to go to bed early on Sunday. We were packed off to bed, making a virtue of the necessity, because we were "played out" and, had we not been able to go to bed, we should have been compelled to sing more hymns.

Now, my own children are inclined to sympathize with me when I tell them this story. I don't ask for their sympathy, and I don't want it. There was a particular value in that kind of liturgical process. It created the rhythm of life—the pulse of life. Once a week our whole attitude to life was first of all authoritatively, and then, more spontaneously transformed. We read what were called religious books on Sunday. We played what was called religious music. And musically we were most grateful for the syncopation of sanctity. We nevertheless were involved in a life for which the regular beat was Christian remembrance. That day has gone. It has not been retained even among those who attend church on Sunday morning, because the value of Sunday in itself has been lost. A secularistic attitude to life as a whole has been put in its place.

For the Protestant, if not for the Catholic, the Christian year has suffered the same eclipse. We now have Mothering Sunday and we shall soon have Fathering Sunday. We have, in the Methodist Church, Christian Citizenship Sunday, and what was "Worn Out Ministers' Sunday" under a more euphonious name, for a Methodist minister may be worn out but nowadays his description is "superannuated". The alteration is best epitomized in the changing of Rogation Sunday, which was part of the Christian year, to Farm Sunday, which is a rural ceremony. There can be no doubt whatsoever that this exercise of remembrance, where it is increasingly separated from the pattern of the Christian year, produces a secularism which is almost unavoidable. We may pity our forefathers who slaved in the fields for a mere pittance, but we would do well to remember that they had between fifty or sixty feast days a year when they did not work. Today we have innumerable secular holidays which do not contribute to anything except loss of life on the roads, and some incidental relaxation for some people who otherwise would find little time for leisure.

This is the basis of our secularism. This is the ground for the claim that the passing of Sunday as a day given over to religious exercises, and the neglect of the Christian year, have produced a situation, in which those to whom we preach are not in any suitable condition to receive what we have to say. The pattern and culture and temper and climate of their lives are set in a secular field.

II

Then there is another phenomenon of which we are all too little aware. It is the difference which exists between the life conscious community in which we now live as compared with the death conscious community in which our fathers lived. I remember as a Sunday School scholar singing a hymn, a tunesome ditty by Sullivan, which reminded me as I sang it of "D'Oyly Carte", in which these words appeared:

> *I'm but a stranger here,*
> *Heaven is my home;*
> *Earth is a desert drear,*
> *Heaven is my home.*

Another passage in this same hymn goes on like this:

> *And time's wild wintry blast*
> *Soon will be over-passed;*

Now those words sound preposterous in our ears. But consult any of the evangelical hymnals of fifty years ago, and you will see to what a large extent the emphasis of preaching was concerned with the next world. And it is not difficult to discover why.

Bertrand Russell in his *History of Western Philosophy* points out that up until about the seventeenth century all thinking was about death. It is only by a strenuous effort of will that you and I can think ourselves back into an environment where most people died before they were thirty-five and death was cheek by jowl with the living all the time. People who fell ill probably died of their ailment. In fact, death was the ever-present reality rather than life. Astounding changes have taken place in your lifetime and mine. The expectation of life is now well over sixty. Most diseases are curable and all will be. I remember so distinctly in the "blitz", when I was partly responsible for looking after those who were bombed out in a large area of London, how few people, if any, anticipated that they were going to be killed. Many were killed, but life consciousness even in that disturbing situation was overwhelmingly stronger than the prospect of death. And if you remove the prospect of imminent death, and the close familiarity with it, a new factor enters for the first time in history into the thinking and attitude of ordinary people.

When I began my ministry, I was appointed to a church in the Old Kent Road to the south-east of London, a road mainly famous or notorious for its public houses. One such went by the extraordinary name of "The World Turned Upside Down", and that was an exact description of the place after eleven o'clock on Saturday night. There was great poverty in the district, and one of its simple dramas, and I am speaking of conditions not much more than thirty years ago, was this.

When a little child was diagnosed as having TB (in those days it was often called "galloping consumption") she would perhaps go to the hospital, for a time. Then the little one would be brought home, and in one of these dreary, sleazy streets off the Old Kent Road a kind of throne-room would be created in the downstairs parlour facing the street. In the summer time the window would be opened. The bed would be put up beside it and the little one would hold court. People coming by would talk to her and give her presents and watch her die. There was no possibility of a cure, nothing more that could be done. A strangely beautiful though somewhat macabre drama.

But those of my acquaintance who are stricken with this disease today look upon it as a transient inconvenience, and are quite sure that it is curable even in advanced stages. This is a not inappropriate illustration of the difference in the hearer today, who looks upon life with avid hope where once he looked upon death as an ever present possibility as well as an inevitable prospect.

There are the widest repercussions from the change. I remember visiting Jamaica not so long ago and reflecting upon the people who live in that most beautiful island, grandchildren of slaves brought over from the continent of Africa in boats bearing the names of Christian martyrs and captained by Christian skippers who read suitable passages from the Old Testament to the wretches herded like cattle in the holds. As I saw the slums of Kingston, which are all the more horrible because of the sophisticated dirt superimposed upon the primitive squalor of native poverty, I remember that it was out of such experiences of inevitable death that they composed those Negro Spirituals, which we so glibly and easily sing,

> *I got shoes, you got shoes,*
> *All God's children got shoes.*
> *When I get to heaven gonna put on my shoes*
> *Gonna walk all over God's heaven.*

But no shoes here, no hope here.

> *I got a robe, you got a robe,*
> *All God's children got robes.*
> *But when I get to heaven gonna put on my robe.*

That expresses the death consciousness of a community which listened respectfully, and sometimes with deep emotion, to the preaching of its time.

Today a slum dweller from Kingston, if he so desires, can quickly cross this delightful island and reach the millionaires' paradise of the north shore—Montego Bay, the haven of rest for exhausted Hollywood film stars. He may get a job in the kitchens of one of the fabulous hotels. If he does he will see more refuse from the tables thrown away in one night than would be required to feed twenty or thirty families for a week in Kingston. He is not now singing his spirituals about the next world. He is waiting for the Communist agent to arrive to tell him about this one—and I don't blame him.

This life conscious emphasis produces an entirely new reaction. If we talk about eternal life, as under God we

17

are compelled to do when we preach, we must talk about the present possibility which our blessed Lord advocated and himself spoke of. Unless we can out-think, and out-speak, and out-live and, if need be, out-die those who offer life with both hands, we shall make little impact upon those whose consciousness of life and all it offers has been enormously increased even in the few years of our own lifetime.

III

There is one other great disposing factor in the attitude of the hearer. I am indebted for an introduction to this theme to a very great British Methodist, Dr. J. Ernest Rattenbury, who began his preaching sixty-five years ago. I once asked him if he would tell me what, in his judgment, was the great difference between the attitude of people in his day, sixty-five years ago, and the attitude today. He had no difficulty in answering. He said, "In any congregation, normal or otherwise, sixty-five years ago, you could count on a general sense of guilt. Now the only thing you can count on is a general sense of doubt."

There is a wealth of wisdom in those words. The profound sense of personal guilt has almost disappeared. We are quite ready to impute guilt to others, preferably to groups, but it makes no powerful individual impact. The general attitude, if not of doubt, is at least one of curiosity and of speculation. This may not be as true of some groups as it is of others. Those who are more fundamentally inclined are more likely to be infused with this sense of guilt even today. But, generally speaking, it is true, and the attitude is likely to spread in the coming days. We have to speak, as preachers, to hearers who are in various stages of doubt.

If we are to deal with the minds and hearts of these doubters we have to begin by recognizing that, partly due to the nature of modern education, and partly due to the spread superficially of forms at least of purported knowledge, there *is* this almost universal epidemic kind of doubt. Whereas once the processes of education were mainly concerned with pushing into the mind a certain number of nourishing facts, the trend of much education today is the promotion of a kind of critique. It is rather like giving a guidebook on stomachic values to people who are in need of a good square meal. But there can be little doubt that this process is far advanced, and consequently the mood is not to regard Christianity as craftsmanship, but much more to regard it as craftiness. Consequently, before we can make any impression upon those to whom we seek to preach today, we have to recognize that they are already in a resistant frame of mind. They have been encouraged to think very largely in terms of doubt, and the more authoritatively we claim to speak, the more likely we are to produce an ambivalent, if not a contrary, effect to that which we desire. This is the outstanding characteristic of the hearer.

It is, I think, at bottom, a loss of a sense of need. One of the curious effects of preaching today seems to be to stimulate an interest in religion in inverse proportion to the need for it. It is so generally and factitously assumed that if we can only get people to church, sooner or later, by some kind of inexorable process, they will become Christians. It is my experience that a great many who are brought to church are thereafter inoculated against the real thing and permanently incapacitated for catching it. Without in any way appearing to be contentious, I would beg to remind you that the various evangelical jamborees in our country, promoted a few years ago by a trans-Atlantic organization, produced immediate effects many of which I've no doubt were good. It would be ill advised to denigrate them beyond saying that there is practically no permanent result from them. But, having said that, it is essential to point out that alongside those who were influenced for the good because they were receptive of a totalitarian presentation of "the Bible says", there were a great many people who were so adversely affected that it is almost impossible for any impact to be made upon them by any other kind of Christian evangelism.

That is, if you do not take account of the state of critical dubiety in which your hearer is, you may produce by the very processes of your evangelical, or other kinds of preaching a result which is nothing short of calamitous. Dubiety is not brought to the point of decision because of the loss of the sense of need. No preaching is of effect if it speaks to a situation which does not exist, and proposes a cure for a disease from which the victim is not conscious that he is suffering. Until you can suggest that you have an answer to the problem which vexes the hearer, you have no point of contact with the hearer, you have no attack whereby you can drive home the claim that you seek to make and offer the answer which you believe Christ has. Nevertheless there is alongside this absence of a sense of need an undoubted increase in curiosity.

Our problem is how we can relate this loss of a sense of need to this undoubted increase in a sense of curiosity. Over the last few years there has been an increase of interest in Christianity on the radio and on television, which is in direct contrast to the sense of profound conviction about it. When I first begun to speak in the open air thirty-four years ago, people were quite ready to talk about political evils, they were quite ready to talk about the inequities of trans-Atlantic and trans-Continental powers, they were perfectly ready to have a go at the parson and to blame the Church, they were quite ready, in fact, to say anything and everything providing you did not endeavour to face them with a religious issue pure and simple. If you did, then they lost interest. It was not their cup of tea. They were not concerned about it. The subject of religion *today*—not only Christianity but other world religions—has come very much to the fore. One of the "surefire" programmes on any television circuit today is a discussion on religion. People will fall over themselves to take part in such discussions and are most anxious to ventilate their own views on such matters. Now this is a fact. In a nutshell, plenty of interest, very little concern.

How are these two matters to be reconciled? The old frontiers and the old bases of thought have largely been eroded and are no longer held with anything like the same consistency. It is this lack of basic ideology which promotes at one and the same time a sense of temporary euphoria and a sense of permanent curiosity. Whereas I can recollect thirty-four years ago the stridency and fervour with which young men professed the Communist case, or others professed the Christian case, or others professed the Socialist case, or others professed the Pacifist case, there has been a gradual withering of these certainties, and in their place has come a wistfulness alongside a sense of personal euphoria. And though it will be untrue to say that we've never had it so good, which was an electioneering slogan very far removed from the truth, it is true that the slogan "I'm all right, Jack", which may also leap across the Atlantic for all I know, is one which expresses this sense of temporary euphoria. It is a reflection of this basic and, I think, utterly constituent element in the state of the hearer.

Whether those who listen today are gathered outside in pagan and non-ecclesiastical surroundings or flock inside to early services on Sunday; whether they belong to the various revival groups that are as manifest in the Catholic as in the non-Catholic Churches; whether they are caught up in the revivals of Islam and of Buddhism; or whether they take part in various attempts to resuscitate the Church by adventitious and somewhat unreasonable methods which can be generally regarded as within the gimmick range, yet it is true that these are the elements of a situation which is likely to become further aggravated. It would be idle to pretend that I think the state of the hearer is going to be changed quickly. What obviously is required is that we must induce a sense of spiritual values. What is obviously required is that we must re-enforce the sense of spiritual power. And, what above all is required, is that we must be able to communicate a sense of true authority. And searching my own conscience and my own experience it would seem to me that the Christian Church, as regards the state of the hearer, is running into more perilous and difficult times than ever. I believe that the city of God remaineth, and I have no ultimate fear. Yet I think the auguries are unfortunate in the sense that the problems are likely to increase and the prevailing mood of secularism and life consciousness and doubt also are likely to increase at least for some long time to come.

CHAPTER II

THE PREPARATION OF THE PREACHER

THE preparation of the preacher for an adequate presentation of the case for Christianity in the contemporary situation is no easy problem. Unless he be an outstanding genius, the condition of the preacher necessarily is already basically determined. The very facts of the condition of the hearer involve a situation from which there is practically no escape.

To begin with, if it be true that there is heterogeneity among the hearers, then it is necessarily true that the preacher will either have to confine himself to talking to one group with which he is familiar, and with which sooner or later he may unfortunately become identified, or else he will be compelled to talk vaguely to a larger group in the hope that he may light upon a suitable pattern of generalities concerning which no precise information that his hearers may have is likely to bear. Now, we will consider for a moment the situation of the preacher who, in order to satisfy his congregation, has to deal with a pattern which is more or less regular and unchanging. The illustrations are historically beyond dispute. It has been said that the Church of England from about the eighteenth century to the middle of the nineteenth was very largely the Tory Party at prayer.

The first part of that is unexceptionable; the second part is dubious, but in general, it is not too far from the truth. It is said of the early days of the Labour Party, with which ideologically I have much more in common, that it was rather like the Methodist Church on the rampage. And that, I think, has a good deal to commend it, particularly in these days when most of the credit for such left-wing policies as emerge from the Labour Party (and they are not necessarily large at the moment) is given to materialistic sources. They probably have much more to do "with Methodism than with Marx". As a contemporary labour leader in England has said, the situation gives some substance to the assertion that the preacher speaks to a more or less conforming group and is required sooner or later to conform thereto himself. This, therefore, alienates him from the totality of the community in which he lives. Unless he is of unusually strong mind or of great piety, he is likely to take the colour of his sermons from the various hues represented by his congregations. It is unfortunately true that a great many preachers speak always and without exception to groups which are more or less taken from particular social, ideological, and intellectual strata. It is well nigh impossible, except for the moral giant, to break entirely through the pattern of conformity in which he is expected to find his place.

On the other hand, if the preacher has the opportunity of speaking to a wider and more heterogeneous congregation, the same problem faces him in reverse. In order to accommodate himself to a congregation in which he dare not speak with precision on matters in which he is a sheer amateur among many professionals, he will be inclined to deal with subjects which are vague and pseudo-spiritual, in the confidence that a great many people who are experts in their own particular field will feel like taking a certain time off once a week to enjoy a kind of temporary excursion into a world which at least has the appearance of spirituality.

This conformity or vagueness does not constitute the most dangerous element in the situation in which the preacher finds himself. Its most dangerous implication is that he becomes an alien figure. It is that he is expected to deal with and to speak of a world which is not the normal over-all pattern of the world in which his hearer lives. Religion becomes if not the escape hatch, then the occasional side-line, the spiritual hobby of people whose main business is to be found elsewhere. This is reflected in the contention so often made that the parson's business —whatever else he does—should be to keep out of politics. For any intervention in the practical affairs of the community in which he lives will be a betrayal of his trust and will, in fact, degrade, if not debauch his ministry.

This is a new form of heresy which would have been utterly inconceivable to any churchman of the Middle Ages, to say nothing to Luther and others. The fact of involvement in the political field was not regarded, until this curious modern era, as any aberration from the proper ministry of the Gospel. I remember how ruefully the immortal Dr. Temple, Archbishop of Canterbury, spoke on a London bomb-site soon after the war, and only a few days before he died. He said to a number of businessmen who were there, "You are a queer lot. You are always asking that the Church should give a lead. Now I came to your Guild-hall the other evening at your invitation and talked to you about the amount of profit that you should make in your economic transactions, and suggested that twenty-five per cent was a conservative figure. And you said, 'Why doesn't the Church mind its own business?' " That ambivalence of attitude is one of the inevitable results of the kind of secularity in which the modern community lives. The parson, if he does become integrated with his fellows, is integrated, not at the spiritual level of his message, but at the social level of his conviviality. And that is one of the major disasters with which we are all confronted as preachers of the Gospel. We use the bonhommie of our social grade, or our athletic prowess, to hide the alienation which divides us from our congregations at the deeper levels of life and work.

This again is part of the wider problem of irrelevancy. The condition which is finally imposed upon the parson today is that he is regarded as saying things and involving himself in notions which are fundamentally irrelevant. I was talking in the open air some years ago, when a man in the crowd, after listening somewhat impatiently for a bit, interjected the comment that he thought I was mad. And he felt that all parsons were mad. I resisted the imputation and said that, on the whole, I thought we were not. But he persisted and, finally, as if to prove his point, he said, "Well, if you're not mad can you prove you're not mad?" Well, I confess I found that a bit difficult. I had never been called upon to prove I wasn't mad before, so, hoping to play for time, I said to him, "Well, can you prove that you're not mad?" He said, "I can." And he did. He produced his discharge certificate from a mental institution. And that most effectively closed the conversation.

But I pondered the matter afterwards and saw that, though he may have put it a little brusquely, what he was saying was not quite so far from the mark as I was pleased to think. After all, what is madness but irrelevancy? If what goes on in my mind has nothing to do with what is going on in the world around me, I am mad. If I live in a private world of my own which has no contact with the world outside me, I am, strictly and clinically, insane. There are a great many people who have no objection to our making pious noises in peculiar places. But they will not grant what we have to say is radically concerned with the kind of life in which they're involved. As far as they are concerned, if we like to play at religion, that's our business. But it butters no parsnips, nothing is fundamentally altered by it. We are, in fact, indulging in a pleasant game which makes no vital impression upon the sort of world in which we live. We are, in fact, irrelevant because what we speak of is a world which is non-existent, and we are irrelevant because we use a language which is unintelligible. Or, if it is not unintelligible, it is the kind of language which is so specialized that dogmatism is the only setting in which it can be advanced.

That, of course, is the prime fallacy as well as function of dogmatism. If you use a strange and irrelevant language, if you deal in mental categories which are remote from the general conceptions of your audience, you must be dogmatic. You cannot argue, in any case, because your hearers have no competence to deal with your arguments; but they have ears to hear and may be suitably impressed by the intensity of your utterings. These are problems which confront the preacher. I have put them deliberately at their blackest because I want to be as sombre as I think is realistic, and to utter as serious a word of warning as to me seems necessary.

Unless this rift is dealt with, the future of preaching is dark. Of course if a man has the love of God in his heart, if he is on fire with Jesus Christ, if he says his prayers and means them, if he is a member, consciously and radically, of the body of Christ, if he yearns to see justice done, if it hurts him when others are dispossessed or disadvantaged, if his heart is on fire with a passion of evangelism and if he desires nothing more than to see the kingdom of God come, then none of these difficulties will disable him. But they will impair his message. And we need more than the faithfulness of those who continue in dark and difficult places to proclaim the Gospel if we are to redress the balance of secularism which is now upon us. Therefore, I want to turn now to those things by which a man may prepare himself as a preacher.

I

I propose to discuss that preparation in three categories —the practical, the intellectual, and the spiritual.

First of all, in no carping spirit, may I remind you of the sorry pass to which preaching has come because of the arrival of the television camera, among other things. Evangelism has become a performance often more reminiscent of Perry Como than of some of the great giants of evangelism. This slipshod method of presentation is geared to conversation rather than to oratory and to preaching. Now I make no bones about it. I am seeking to be a champion of high oratory. It may be unfashionable, but I am not a preacher of fashion; neither should you be. I do not believe that the day of vehement, effective, even flamboyant oratory is gone. If it has gone, the sooner we recapture it the better. For the dimension of oratory is one of the necessary dimensions of effective evangelism, and effective preaching, in general.

I am not hoping to reinaugurate the rotund kind of oratory beloved of the late Dr. Parker of City Temple. In any case it would not survive long in our present generation. I am not asking for the kind of oratory which is a mixture of exhibitionism and totalitarianism. I am asking that in the practical sphere we should remember that we can harness dramatic ability to the presentation of the Gospel, and as preachers so we ought to do. How many of us have fallen into the quite erroneous and somewhat blasphemous assumption that if you take care of the substance of what you have to say the good Lord will take care of your larynx. How many assume that the mere possession of a fervour for righteousness will equip the preacher with the gifts necessary to communicate that fervour to his congregation.

Those who belong to the dramatic profession in England cannot understand how this situation has been allowed to develop in the Church. I remember a conversation with a dramatic actor, who is in charge of one of the major and most influential drama schools in London. He sometimes attends my meetings in Hyde Park. One afternoon he buttonholed me when I got down from the rostrum and said to me that he was very glad that he'd had the opportunity of coming to the meeting, which I thought was kind of him, and then he went on to say, "You know, we would never allow a man to go on the stage and take part in a play just because he knew his lines. We require him to make himself competent so to put them across as to give them their optimum effect. And yet you preachers seem to think that such an exercise is, if not degrading, certainly unnecessary." I believe that dramatic actor put his finger on a really important point. I wonder how many preachers have any knowledge, or had any knowledge before the tape recorder came into being, of the sound of their own voice? I wonder how many preachers have any knowledge of their appearance in full flight of oratory? I wonder how many preachers have any realistic idea of their physical postures in the process?

"Most gestures," said the immortal Sarah Bernhardt,

"made by the amateur speaker are involuntary methods of preventing himself from falling over." I believe that that is cruelly but substantially true. It may be that your gestures are comely and elegant. It may be that they are idiosyncratic and peculiar. But certainly you should find out. I have learned that one of the reasons why people do not habitually listen to open air speakers is that they have a healthy desire not to watch another man suffering. To give the appearance of suffering in the pulpit, or at the street corner, is not the best commendation of the joyful news. These are not trivialities. We ought to be for Christ's sake as good artisans and craftsmen as are those who work upon the secular stages for the entertainment of their fellows. Unless we can enhance and enrich our message with the craftsmanship of good Christian acting we shall be failing in our task.

Even in the matter of enunciation we often fail. It is impossible ultimately to speak without opening the mouth, and yet there are a great many people who make the endeavour. It is impossible to speak effectively without knowing the cadence and use of words in their proper context. In this respect we have much to learn from the silver screen. The late and much lamented Humphrey Bogart was a master of the art of throwing away the words "that don't matter". One of the secrets of being able to sustain the interest of a congregation which is not addicted to righteousness and feels somewhat out of touch with Christian affairs anyhow, is found in the emphasis given to the words that are important and the throwing away of the words that are not. For there is nothing more tedious than the rhythmic beat of each successive syllable.

This is a problem which deserves careful investigation. Let me commend it to you as part of our bounden duty in Christ. It will involve a discipline which may not be pleasant to begin with, but will be fruitful in the end. We have no right to become less effective in our field of advocacy than the trained technicians and experts are in the various fields of television. How few are those who have the correct embouchure and aplomb for public oratory, or have taken enough trouble to make sure that their own qualifications are submitted to the rigour and the regimen of the television screen. Here is part of our practical, and I believe, inevitable preparation.

There are two things to be added. The appearance of a preacher cannot be a matter of indifference. There is no particular piety or tradition attached to the cassock which I wear. There is, however, a virtue in the wearing of a recognizable habit. The mantle of the prophet may be an occasional mantle. The vesture of the priest needs to be much more regular and unmistakable.

There is one other practical consideration. If, in the attempt to regain that kind of relationship with the congregation which has been lost, a preacher is required to enter into controversial matters, it is of the utmost importance that he should endeavour to secure two pulpits in his ministry. Otherwise, he will be compelled to funnel through one pulpit all that he has to say. There will be those who come to be fed with the bread of life who may be regaled with some controversial issue; and there will be others who are looking for guidance in complex matters who will resent the fact that there is no room for the inclusion of intelligent and Christlike discussion on those themes. My own situation is most fortunate. I am relieved of any necessity to try to deal with controversial issues on Sunday morning because I have an ample opportunity of doing it in another place on Sunday afternoon. Those who wish to be *en rapport* with their congregations, and preach in such a way as to come before their hearers not only with sincerity but with power, should find the opportunity of dissociating the purely evangelical and nourishing part of their ministry from that which must be necessarily educational and provocative.

II

What should be our preparation in the intellectual field? When I came down from Cambridge I was sent to the Old Kent Road and therefrom I went to Tower Hill. Tower Hill is a kind of Mars Hill of London's dinner hour. When I first stood on a wall and suggested that if my hearers would like to ask a question I would try to answer it, I had already prepared answers to questions about Church history. I had prepared an answer to the question, who was Cain's wife? I had made some lucubrations in the realm of Greek and Hebrew and I had excerpts from a number of sermons tucked up my sleeve. I felt that I was more or less equipped for the task.

The first question I was asked was about Karl Marx, and I'd never heard of him. Or, if I'd heard of him, he was very remote and I knew next to nothing about him. I had to say to the heckler that it was a tricky question and I'd tell him next week. I went home and rang up some of the pundits of the Methodist Church, but they'd never heard of Karl Marx either. Eventually I borrowed some literature and I began to read. It taught me a paramount lesson. If a preacher is to be prepared he must begin where his congregation is and not where he'd like his hearers to be. Unless we are properly apprised of where they are, we shall probably turn our ministry into an excellent institution for answering the questions that nobody is asking. It is, therefore, of supreme importance in the intellectual preparation of the preacher that he should acquaint himself with the point at which his hearers are, and begin from there, and not from uninformed assumptions about their situation.

This is a difficulty which is likely to become more intense and which necessarily will involve all sorts of questions, some more acute and some more profound. But, if we are not prepared by knowing more or less where our congregation starts, we shall be in grave danger of never making contact with them at all. Yet it is not so difficult as it sounds, because there are whole areas where there are common interests furnishing opportunities for the presentation of the Gospel.

Intellectually our second great difficulty is that of vocabulary. I am not a logical positivist. As a satisfactory theory of knowledge it seems to me to be open to the gravest objections. At the same time I am grateful to the linguistic philosophers for their emphasis upon a problem ignored by the majority of standard philosophers. Words are the only precise means of communication we have, and there is danger of assuming that familiarity gives them explicability. Whereas the highly probable fact is that many of the words we use are not relevant because they are unspecific. Much of the language in which the Christian Gospel is at present advanced is language which, by linguistic tests, is imprecise, irrelevant, and insignificant. In fact, it has no point of contact with reality.

As an example linguistically speaking, it is significant to say that Jesus was a man, whereas it is insignificant to say that Jesus was divine. That is a bold statement. I think it is nevertheless a true one. I am prepared to say that Jesus is divine. I believe it from the bottom of my heart. But in preaching we dare not assume that there is some connotation attached to the idea of the divinity of Jesus as there is to the idea of his manhood. This is a continuing and exacerbating difficulty. The problem for us is whether or not we are addicted to a form of words which itself is imprecise and useless. We must insistently ask ourselves: What do those who hear us understand by the words we use?

Frequently our vocabulary is too limited. One of the golden rules for effective preaching is the enlargement of vocabulary so that we are not confined to general purpose words like fellowship, a word which ought to be expunged from all oratory about Christianity along with others of a similar ambiguity. We use such words in various contexts for lack of others more precise and meaningful. There is nothing more fruitful for a young preacher than to learn at least one new word each day, so that he may vary what he has to say, thus avoiding monotony and increasing impact upon those who hear.

The problem does not lie only in the limited vocabulary from which we suffer. It lies also in a vocabulary which itself is inadequate to the tasks we have to perform, and far from being an explication of our case constitutes very largely an evasion of it.

A further word needs to be said about illustrations. They only very rarely serve to illustrate. Or if they do, they quite often illustrate the very opposite of what we intend. When I was a boy at Sunday School I remember first hearing the story of David and Goliath. I was intended to support David, but my sympathies were entirely with Goliath. Here was a man cluttered up with about two tons of armour and only able to move at about four miles an hour. He was threatened by a young man throwing stones from a safe distance, who finally stunned the poor fellow and while he was unconscious cut his head off. That does not connote for me great bravery. It only indicates low cunning and an unerring aim with a stone. Yet, almost invariably we assume that a biblical analogy will be edifying, and as an illustration must adorn the Christian argument. It is a dangerous fallacy.

The kind of illustration which is of value is that which can spring out of the preacher's own experience as indicative of the way in which he himself was brought to a better understanding of the particular issue with which he is attempting to deal. Here is an illustration which I think is pertinent, and the kind of illustration which is effective. I was confronted with a large and menacing crowd many years ago talking to me in strident terms about the evils of a coal strike. One of the men in the crowd (I'm pretty sure he wasn't a local preacher of the Methodist Church) cried out in a very loud and threatening voice, "What do you think of the wage solution that has been offered for our claim?" It was in the days when miners were cruelly treated. It was in the days when Aneurin Bevan was still smarting under the capitalist perversion of the Sankey Report which in 1918 advocated the nationalization of the mines. It was in the days when there was much more poverty than there is now. I heard his question and I replied to it. I said, "I believe, my friend, in the inviolability of human personality," which I thought was pretty good. He cried, "So what?" And I was ashamed. You see, what is the inviolability of human personality? It's like the stewardship of wealth, or the companionship of industry, or the brotherhood of man, and all the miserable rigmarole of ambiguities which may comfort us and yet annoy to the point of frustration those who have no particular interest in our clichés.

If we are to make intellectual contact with those to whom we fain would speak in the name of Christ today, in God's name let us say what we mean. Let us say it with what eloquence we can command, with what erudition we can bring to it, and with what precision the good Lord will give us.

III

The last form of preparation is spiritual preparation. The true preparation for the preaching of the Gospel is the possession of the golden secret of the love of God, a personal experience of forgiveness of sins, and an overwhelming desire to communicate that experience to others that they too may come to the saving grace of their Lord and ours. But within that broad category there are certain qualities which are peculiarly required.

The most disabling threat to evangelistic success is the conviction of many people that we parsons are not quite as honest in our pulpits as most scientists are in their laboratories or teachers are in their classrooms. If that kind of criticism can be well and truly made then not only will the Christian preacher be discredited, but for the time being his message will be discredited, too. Many people have the feeling that we are above all concerned not to "flutter the dovecotes", not to disturb the simple faith of those who come to church, not to take away, even if it is something that is ultimately untrue, what they have so long cherished. I believe that is not only fundamentally cowardice, I believe it is mercenary. There is nothing which destroys the integrity of the Church so much as the assumption that it is playing a little with the truth.

I am not one who spends his time looking around for odd crumbs of comfort the scientists may drop from their table, and which we may gratefully pick up. There is something quite ignoble and unworthy in waiting on the scientist, hoping that he will be kindlier than were his fathers. At the same time, there is one quality which seems to me to shine like a beacon from the laboratories of this and every country, not least of all the U.S.S.R. And it is the clinical, limpid, splendid honesty with which scientists will say only those things for which they have compelling evidence. They will not advance a claim until they have built up inductively a case which they believe to be overwhelming. Some of them think that what we do is to say things for the good of people's souls which, on evidence otherwise discovered, we know to be untrue. That is an exaggeration, as perhaps my commendation of the scientist is slightly in advance of the facts. But there is the trend and there is the peril.

This is the other side of the problem of which the reverse is the kind of doubt in which our congregations live. Those who preach the word have many doubts. The false parade of our assurance on matters which are in grave doubt is, as I have been arguing, one of the most menacing of all the problems with which we are confronted. When I began my ministry I was trying to hold on to about 350 different theological propositions. I felt like Stephen Leacock, who described his hero as jumping on his horse and riding off in all directions at once. Now I am much older, and perhaps not so silly, I believe about three things. But, whereas I was strenuously endeavouring to hold on to a number of propositions thirty years ago, now I can say without truculence and certainly without any kind of impropriety the truths I know *hold me*, and I am content to be dubious about many other things. If we are to be honest it may cut down by a very large degree the number of topics on which we expatiate. But it will enhance the value of those things which we can so speak of, as to infuse into those who hear us a sense of the same vital and absolute assurance, personal certitude if not objective certainty, with which we hold them. It depends, of course, ecclesiastically on the particular communion to which we belong as to what will be required as the irreducible minimum. I would respectfully suggest that the minimum in many cases is too high.

A great many of the things which we have relegated to the realm of belief can be more properly found in the realm of positive action. But honesty, honesty now, honesty all the time. Let it be said that you do not make enemies by being honest. If you speak with charity you may make a bond which links you with those among your hearers who disagree with you. You make enemies, or at least you fail to make friends for Christ's sake, if there is a general dust and cloud of insincerity blown up by your words.

Dr. Schweitzer has expressed for our generation the idea of respect for personality. Nothing is more imperative than that we should not abuse the opportunity which comes to us; that we should never regard our congregations and our hearers as means to an end, but invariably as ends in themselves. Much of the time we ask too much and we ask it too soon. If we are to respect those who come to us we must at all costs avoid the sin of pride. It would be a sorry ministry and a sorry priesthood which did not covet believers in the things which it holds dear and therefore seek to impart those treasures to others who have them not. There is a sacredness about the ministry and there is an eternity about the Church. How heartily do I agree that there is no salvation outside the body of Christ. But within that body we are members one of another, and our ministry consists in the recognition first and last and always that we are in the sight of God of equal and eternal value.

And now a last word. Our spiritual preparation must be in the pattern of our Lord. And it follows simply that that pattern must be seen first of all in the way in which our blessed Lord conducted his own personal ministry, the way in which he taught and spoke and acted. We know a good deal about his ministry. We know how he begun it. We know of the severely practical way in which he took the old prophecy and proclaimed its fulfilment. "Today hath this scripture been fulfilled in your ears." We also know from evidence which is irrefragable the method our Lord applied. It is seen in the strictest contrast if we think of the attempts that many of the Greek teachers made to come to terms with ultimate reality. Many of them began with the *ultimate* and endeavoured therefrom to come by slow and easy stages to the known and the simple. To begin with the first mover, the prime mover, and, thereafter, to come to an understanding of the nature of man. Our Lord began in entirely the opposite way. He did not begin with the unknown and then endeavour to reduce the terms of that ignorance about the ultimate to terms of knowledge and familiarity. He began with the things that were known. In fact, he began spiritually where people were. He talked to farmers about their crops and showed that there was a clear relationship between the natural law and the spiritual world. He talked to housewives about a piece of coin or jewellery lost and the house turned upside down to find it. He talked to ordinary people about the known and recognizable qualities which they at their best demonstrated. And sometime his illustrations were, to say the least of it, picaresque. You will remember the story, for instance, of the man knocked up at midnight by one who wanted to borrow something. Our Lord suggested that had the man not continued to knock he certainly would have had no bread. Because, however, he continued to knock, the householder said, "Well if he goes on knocking he'll wake the children up and nobody will have any sleep," and he got what he wanted. "How much more shall God give good things to them that ask Him," said Jesus. He told the story of the unfortunate widow and the judge who was no better than he should be. He told these stories alongside the parables, which are not extraordinary tales of remarkable events but simple tales of what went on. Upon that foundation, which established immediate rapport with those to whom he spoke, he raised the magnificent super-structure of his own thought about the kingdom and the requirements of those who would enter it.

Here is unmistakable evidence of a supreme preaching technique and of a supreme teacher. Here is the practical business of preaching alongside an inter-penetrating but glorious Gospel of the love of God and the magnificent structure of ultimate truth. And so it must be with us. Building upon that rock we shall, by the grace of God, erect a house of evangelism which will not only withstand the shocks of the tempest, but will be the mansion in which many will gather for comfort until it becomes the household of God.

CHAPTER III

THE ARENA OF PREACHING

If it is a fact that we cannot count on the immediacy of a sense of sin, and have to begin further back, as it were, to establish contact with those with whom we would reason for Christ's sake, then it follows that preaching is an arena in which the confrontation must first be in terms of ideas or of problems rather than of the sinful soul with the challenge and offer of Christ. The Christian Church cannot be an institution for answering the questions nobody is asking. In order that we may come later on to that evangelical emphasis and challenge which is our prime or our fundamental business, we have to begin with the challenge of our years, however inchoate, imprecise, unordered and invalid its ideas may be. It is there that we can expect to find a point of contact, and it is there that we must begin today. And if we would make our advocacy in terms of questions which are at least implicit in people's minds, rather than needs which are rampant in their souls, then we can, with propriety, start with the challenge of none other than Lenin himself. Lenin, knowing only partially the truth of his observation, said that Christianity must either overcome Communism or Communism would overcome Christianity. It is perfectly clear that, in the narrower sense, no Christian can be a Communist, and indeed thorough opposition to Communism as an ideology must be the profession of his faith. The real problem, however, the confrontation of ideas, does not lie in the precise and academic and classical presentation of the Communist case. Communism has attracted to itself the basic alternative ideas, or the basic challenges of the mind, with which we as Christians must deal if we are to come to grips with those to whom we would preach Christ.

It is obviously true, as Bertrand Russell says, that the examination of the processes of history by the dialectical method is valuable. It is equally obvious that there has been a large and continuous process in Russia itself of withdrawal from some Communist beliefs, and a forgetfulness which is either conscious or unconscious about many others. The proletarian dictatorship has not come to pass, the withering away of the State has not come to pass, and the emergence of the personality cult, though denied in words by Krushchev, is maintained in practice. The second and equally important element in the Communist classics, the Labour Theory of Value, is hardly mentioned today, and does not in fact maintain anything more than an academic and museum interest. The programme of action as laid down, not so much by Marx but by Lenin and his followers, has similarly been almost entirely repudiated, in words if not in principle, by none other than Krushchev. His assertion of the necessity of competitive co-existence has no place in the Communist canon and is directly and absolutely contrary to the Marxist principle. It is important that those of us who are attempting to say that Christianity is superior to

Communism ideologically should be in possession of these enheartening facts.

It is all the more important to be enheartened by them in order that we may face facts which are much less enheartening, and in fact constitute the true menace, or shall we say the true challenge, of the Communist position. I think that challenge can be found in three areas. In the first place, it is to be found not in economics but in politics. What harrasses, vexes, and exasperates the uninstructed as well as the instructed mind of our time is the juxtaposition of the Christian claim of the omnipotence of God, and the Communist claim of the omnicompetence of politics. This is the first and tremendous challenge with which we have to come to terms. It has always been the claim of the Christian Church that the blood of the martyrs is the seed of the Church. That is all very well provided that the martyrs bleed. But modern political propaganda and power can make sure that they don't bleed. They just confess, and there is no objective virtue in the "confession" of a broken Mindzenti who goes into prison with his head high and the announcement that he is not to be believed when he comes out, and after the familiar and nauseating treatment of brainwashing, etc., comes out a caricature of a man, no longer in command of the shining Christian virtues.

Here in perhaps its most critical, active form is the omnicompetence of politics. With the apparatus at its command, and with its immense, novel, and unprecedented resources, it presents a challenge which is not confined merely to the physical or even to the mental realm. How many were the years, and how wearisome they were, in which we imagined that the day was not too far distant when liberation would come to the poor, squalid, dispirited, downhearted Russians who were waiting for their day of release. We comforted ourselves with the reflection that, at least in the intellectual sphere, these moronic victims of oppression would have nothing to offer which we could not better. Then along came the Sputniks and the Luniks. Now we are confronted with the fact that through the agency of an institution which in many respects is evil and reprehensible, there have been amazing achievements not only in the physical but also in the intellectual field, comparable to the best achievements elsewhere.

But that is not the end of the story. It would be difficult if not impossible to demonstrate that there is a perceptibily higher moral standard in the United States, where most people go to church, than there is in England, where most people do not, or that both can show a higher moral standard as against a community in Russia where very few go to church. I think the evidence, and I say this with due care, as far as it is available to me, is that in many respects there is a higher sense of community morals in the Communist areas than there is in some of the non-Communist areas. I am bound to pay my tribute to the sense of responsibility and vocational zeal which struck me like a fresh wind in various satellite countries I visited as well as Russia. This constitutes the pre-eminent challenge of what we call Communism. It is unnecessary, apparently, to believe in God, because those prerogatives of authority and power which we believe to be His, and which by transaction of grace become ours, those blessings, those gifts, can be in fact achieved by other means. This is the first challenge of the Communist argument.

The second challenge, though like it, is not identical. A book has just been written in England by Barbara Wootten, called *Social Science and Social Pathology*. It is an interesting book. It may be a definitive one. It is an extensive attempt to weigh up the social conditions which underlie and perhaps determine the behaviour, delinquent and otherwise, of those that come before the courts and who are officially treated for deficiencies, principally moral deficiencies. At the end of this very lengthy and somewhat diffuse document, the author says that, just as in the nineteenth century Darwinism overthrew the theology of the Church, so today the principles of social science may well overthrow the moral claims of the Christian faith. Now, I think she is wrong, but I am bound to add that there is a suspicion in the minds of a great many people who have not been able to put it succinctly into words, that this is in fact happening. A young doctor I know is at this moment undertaking research in the field of neurology. He is now experimenting with a drug which he says produces penitence. He is not trifling with the truth, but is deeply concerned about the powers which lie in the pharmacopoeia for producing at least the simulacrum of those very conditions which we have so jealously guarded as being matters of pure morality, certainly not of materialistic origin. The challenge of science and social pathology is essentially the same as that offered by the quarters of the earth which are under the domination or the blessings of Communism. A materialistic basis to life progressively bows off the stage spiritual ideas for which there no longer seems to be even a walking-on part.

This challenge has to be met. It has to be met because, particularly in the more advanced economically blessed countries, the manifest advantages and blessings of material prosperity can quite easily obscure the sense of need which otherwise might arise for the love of God, or for the forgiveness of God.

In the realm of power Communism has likewise created a new dimension, and has prompted or has provoked the rest of the world into what it imagines to be suitable reactions. We are obsessed, bedevilled, hag-ridden by the problem of power, which finds its supreme representation in the mushroom cloud of the Hydrogen Bomb.

This problem of power, which is the overshadowing and principal element in the Communist challenge, is seen not as something which is spiritually engendered or even spiritually used, but as something which is within the control of atomic scientists to produce at will, and to exercise for the achievement of any result that may be desired.

If preaching today is to be rehabilitated where it is in disrepair, it must confront the tripartite threat of political omnicompetence, the achievement of materialistic sufficiency, and the emergence of a new concept of power. It is not sufficient to say, "Well that may be true of certain sophisticated congregations or would-be congregations, but it is certainly not true of the congregation to which I minister." In fact it is the atmosphere, it is part of the climate of most congregations today, and will become increasingly the climate in more. I would venture then to try to answer, or to suggest an approach to the answer, to these three problems, beginning first of all with that which is represented in the general concept of the omnicompetence of politics.

I

The first approach to that answer is suggested by the fact that both Dr. Inge and Dr. Temple have variously said that of all the world's religions, Christianity is the most materialistic. Where those two worthies agree, I think you have a working model of infallibility. What they are saying is not that Christianity is rooted in materialism, but that it is concerned with life rather than with that fractional part of it—if that indeed is not a misnomer—which we call the soul. It is that the Christian faith is first concerned to obey the Lord's injunction to seek the Kingdom of God and its righteousness, not to seek the pleasant feelings of conversion, not to seek the prospect of personal bliss hereafter, but first and above all to seek the Kingdom of God. Recall the words with which our Lord began his public ministry. "And he went, as his custom was, on the Sabbath Day into the synagogue to preach, and there was delivered unto him the book of the prophet Isaiah. And he opened the book, and found the place where it was written, The Spirit of the Lord is upon me because he anointed me to preach good tidings to the poor—the opening of the prison house to them is a bond—to proclaim the acceptable year of the Lord. He closed the book and gave it back to the attendant and sat down. The eyes of all in the synagogue were fastened on him and he began to say unto them. Today hath this scripture been fulfilled in your ears" (Luke 4 : 16–19).

Such is the authentic beginning of the public ministry of our Lord, and it is set out in practical and simple terms. It is the fulfilment of the heart-felt wish of a dependent, degraded, oppressed people, offering them the material blessings for which they had longed for so many years, offering them the blessings which they had been denied because the enemy was just over the hill, or indeed within their midst. It is this concept of the Kingdom of God which has been so neglected as to permit the Communist to arrogate to himself the powers which once belonged to the Christian Church. Had such powers been properly exercised the Communist case would have nothing like the appeal it now has, nor would the overtones of the Communist case have anything like the persuasiveness they now possess. Is it not true that were the Kingdom of God to come a great many professing Christians would not recognize it? Is it not true that unless we can provide some presentation in contemporary thought of what the Kingdom of God is like, fewer and fewer will be interested in the arrangement of the furniture in the next world? It is in this realm that we have to begin to do the kind of thinking which hitherto has been very largely taken up by those who profess no spiritual allegiance such as I would claim and such as I would desire.

It is not that we have a Gospel which is intrinsically personal, but which may have social implications. It is that the very nature of our Gospel is both personal and social. We have to regain the initiative which has been temporarily snatched from us by those communities who have a total view of life as community, whereas we have an atomistic and disconnected view of life in terms of personal evangelism or of personal piety. This is all the more important because in so many respects the accredited virtues of the Christian life do not have the same proportion to those who witness them as to those who claim them. I must confess that of a number of people who have told me they were converted, I liked many of them a good deal better before it happened. That is not cynicism. The fact is that over an ever-increasing area of life today the whole emphasis is turning from preoccupation with personal behaviour and is fixing on the explosive power of the new affection of the corporate good as being the best prophylactic and the best antiseptic, and even the best "talcum powder".

The issue can be represented in the context of a good deal of Methodist social witness over the last fifty years. As far as I can remember the kind of behaviour which for me was Christian as a lad was to avoid drinking, to avoid gambling and not to swear. The impression may be due to my imperfect reception of what was said, but I have shared my recollections with others of my own age group and I.Q., and they seem to agree that that also is the impression they retain. Now I am still a teetotaler, though I do not regard alcohol as the devil in solution, and I am prepared to find a place for it, or at any rate for light wines, in the Kingdom of Heaven. That will give no immediate comfort to anybody. But I am quite sure that any man who gambles, if he is a left-winger, is a hypocrite. The socialist who gambles is a hypocrite because gambling is the gathering of sums of wealth into large packets and distributing them according to chance, whereas socialism is the gathering of wealth into small packets and distributing them according to need. I do not often swear, but I think there is a place for strong, if not intemperate, language. But I find that in the world in which I now live or seek to live, my own children are deeply concerned about Apartheid but don't really know the difference between Cydrax and cider. I find that my own children are deeply concerned to march from Aldermaston in protest against continued nuclear testing, but are quite indifferent to the virtues or demerits of football pools.

I find that, in fact, the only kind of real enthusiasm for morality is the one which is geared to a community objective and is not at all set within a personal framework. I know that our bodies are the temples of the Holy Spirit, and I quite agree that in the last stages of preaching we have to present the naked soul of the sinner before the judgment seat of God. But if we are to begin the process of preaching and so to awaken a sense of morality, that morality must be set within the framework of a world in which two out of three people still do not have enough to eat. If you and I have had a fairly adequate breakfast this morning, we are in a minority in the world, a world in which places like Auschwitz exist. I went to Auschwitz. I shall never forget it as a place of horror, the greater the horror because those who perpetrated the most savage and inhuman outrages were in many cases fellow prisoners. I saw the vast squirrel like accumulations of the German authorities, a whole side of a barn enclosing a mountain of human hair, and, even more heartrending, a great storehouse entirely filled with the shoes of tiny children. These are things which bring me to penitence. These are the matters upon which we can depend if we are to bring to our community today a sense of the moral values and the overwhelming case for the good life.

It is in this regard that the Communist challenge has to be met. It is the business of the Church today, as it was the achievement of the Church in the first century, to out-think, outspeak, outdo, and, if need be, outdie its heathen contemporaries. The answer to the omnicompetence of the Communists is the achievement of the Christian in the same field, by weapons and by methods which are commensurate with the dignity of man and which are permissible in the spirit of Christ.

II

The second field, which is just as important and dangerous, is the field of moral values. We must admit the unprecedented achievements in moral conditions that stem from the surgery of the doctor as well as the headmaster's study or the minister's counselling chamber.

Perhaps the greatest of all our needs is summed up in the question, "Who shall guard the guard?" If it be true that within the fabric of our modern society there is power, dominant, surging and ever increasing, then that power may well fall under the condemnation of the immortal Acton's dictum that it may corrupt as it becomes greater, and as it becomes total it may totally corrupt.

We do not as frequently remember that the next sentence in Lord Acton's aphorism was, "All great men are bad." That is a piece of personal cynicism which is not true. But it reminds us that what is supremely necessary in the world today is that those who exercise the hitherto unparalleled power of our age should be those who have the welfare of their fellow creatures at heart. In this regard I would quote my own experience again. Many years ago a man in the open air said to me, "You give me ten minutes on your platform and I will polish off your argument for you." I was a little less cautious then than I am now, and I let him mount the platform and this is what he said: "The Bible is not true. Jesus never lived, and God does not exist." Having got that perilous stuff off his chest he went on to say, "And look at your Christian Churches—all divided up into sects." I forget the number he mentioned, but it was well under the actual figure. He said, "And look at the way you behave. You are always at each other's throats and you are always bickering and always quarrelling. But Jesus was a poor man, Jesus went about doing good, and Jesus was crucified by the capitalists." He said, "That's why I am an atheist."

It was not. The interesting thing was that when he began to criticize the Church, the yardstick by which he made his criticism was this same Jesus who he professed had never lived. There is a sense in which the chickens of rationalism now come home to roost. Krushchev is continuously reminding others of the words of Jesus and protested bitterly in France that they took the holy vessels from the altar when he entered in order to keep God away from him. Now, he is an extremely able man and an extremely dangerous one, particularly with whom to argue. But what is so important is that in this respect the claims by which we are judged are the claims which never could have been made had Jesus not lived. There is no other yardstick. Do you doubt my word? Then may I refer you to the laws about personal behaviour, which are entrenched in the Soviet Constitution at this moment. You will find, for instance, that the laws with regard to marriage, and the laws with regard to abortion, and the laws with regard to illegitimacy, the laws with regard to the various perversions of moral behaviour, were first of all couched in what they regarded as non-Christian categories. Yet you will find today, that the standards by which public morality is judged in the Soviet Union would have been impossible had it not been for One who walked the land of Galilee and hung upon a cross and rose from the grave on Easter Day. Here is our claim, and here is the point of our own appeal. Here is the way in which we can present it to those who come to us with this miasma of doubt created by the Communist presentation of moral capacity. It is true, we do not deny it—how can we deny it?—the ministries of God are not restricted to those who wield spiritual authority. Every good thing is under obligation to his eternal power. But ultimately the standard and pattern of the good life is seen in Christ. Where else will the standard be found?

I had the privilege some years ago of visiting Ceylon and going to see the temple which enshrines the Buddha's tooth. I saw the tooth. The Buddha must have been a very large man. After seeing the tooth I had the privilege of about a couple of hours conversation with one of the greatest saints I think I ever met. He was a Buddhist priest, and I came away from there with a sense of humility which I have retained ever since, but with one strongly impressed conviction which I have not lost yet. The world renouncing faith of the Buddhists may indeed provide a way of sanctity and purity; but only a world embracing faith can lift up a cross. Those who have the greatest power do find that the waters of the earth fail, and that they must root their authority in some concept or other of ultimate and eternal good. I have nothing but confidence that the good which is to be found in our blessed Lord will ultimately triumph because, though it is a dogmatic assertion, it is an increasing experience, that we are "made for God and our souls are restless until they rest in him".

III

One other consideration falls into the last category. Here the issue seems to me to be doubly significant. It is that we are seeing in our generation the fulfilment of the words of our Lord, those who take the sword will perish by it.

Let me give you a personal and an English reaction to the problem of power as it is ultimately expressed by the Hydrogen Bomb. We live on what is regarded by some people as an expendable aircraft carrier off the coast of Europe. We are an occupied country. We are a second rate, if not a third rate power, and we have long since given up the idea that the Kingdom of God is the same thing as the British Empire. These are disagreeable facts. I record them because it is important that we should see what in fact is the nature of power; and in the country from which I come the nature of power has become a pressing, a demanding, an inexorable thought. We knew what it was to be the big brother who not only watched over his junior brothers but told them what to do. We are now at the receiving end of the process. America exercises almost a complete *Imperium in imperio* in England. Many of its military installations are complete in themselves. They have their own churches, their own schools, their own hospitals, within the barbed wire. Finally they have their own bowling alleys; I suppose that is the ultimate in self-sufficiency.

What sparked off a new intensity of feeling about the American military installations was the somewhat ambiguous announcement not so long ago that a radar system was to be set up in Yorkshire which would give two and one half minutes warning of an approaching atomic missile. We felt that two and one half minutes was a bit short. Then we were told that it wasn't really on our behalf this radar system was to be set up, but on behalf of the U.S.A. where they will have fifteen minutes warning. We reflected that though it would be difficult to evacuate London in, say, two and one half minutes, Americans with their customary bustle might do a very great deal in a quarter of an hour for New York. Then we felt that this was all a form of insanity, and we went back to our natural gloom on these matters. That is the mood in which you will find many an Englishman today, and it is the mood in which he not only listens to the parson, but also to the politician. It is a mood in which he is usually inclined to reject both.

I cannot avoid what is obviously controversial, but is to me the most important and vital element in the arena of preaching. I began many years ago to be a Pacifist. I was one of the first of the peace army. Dick Sheppard, of immortal memory, offered with others to go and stand between the Japanese and the Chinese at Chopei, and he called for volunteers. The first volunteer was a general who had learned his business from the Black and Tans in Ireland. The second was Maude Royden, that incomparable woman preacher. The third was Dr. Herbert Gray. The fourth was myself. We were strong in generals. We were a little short of the lower ranks and we never got further than Tilbury docks. But our intentions were good, and we were regarded with a certain amount of sympathy while being subjected to a good deal of ridicule.

Those days have gone. Since those days all kinds of things have happened, particularly a Second World War, and there are some of us who have felt compelled to take a far deeper concern than opposition to war itself. In fact, I come increasingly to the conviction that the differentia of Christianity does not lie in its monopoly of goodness. El Gazali was every bit as good a Moslem saint as St. Francis of Assisi was a Christian. It does not even lie in the formal presentation of theological dogma, because Lenin's definition of matter is almost identical with Thomas Aquinas' definition of God. But it does lie in an attitude to violence. The suffering love of Jesus is the unique and determining distinction. In fact, it is violence and not war with which we are concerned. It is in this regard that beginning with an antipathy to war as I did as a young man, and taking the Pacifist position, I felt compelled to go further. It enlightened and inspired my own convictions with regard to capital punishment. It turned me into a Socialist because there is nothing so nakedly violent as a system based on what we describe as enlightened self-interest. This is only a baptismal name for selfishness. It is expressed in the whole collection of sports which are called blood sports. It is expressed in the whole attitude which is taken to violence *per se*, as if the requirements of true manhood demand something approaching an Allan Ladd or some of the even less intelligent representatives of the cowboy world. Not to be flippant, but merely to record a fact, one of the problems I have pastorally with dear old ladies in my congregation is that many of them are becoming addicted to watching boxing on television, gloves, ring, spitoons, and all.

The insidious nature of violence is represented not

least in the behaviour of our children. It is characterized by the typical sort of film which we see and the typical kind of paperback which is offered for our consumption upon the station bookstall. We are confronted with this turntable view of violence which in itself is the reflection of the whole Communist world. It is to me significant that, for utilitarian reasons rather than, shall we say, for moral ones, there is a disposition, at least in words, for representatives of the power of Communism to begin to discredit the very means of power which they have so inextricably and often violently exercised. It is in this regard that I have personally been compelled to make certain decisions, and I would be less than honest if I did not pass them on to you. I have felt compelled to become a vegetarian. It would do you all good, but I am not making this a substantial point. Of course there is a complex problem in which compromise is essential, and I am a little concerned about my leather shoes. Whatever may be the Christian attitude to some of these borderline expressions of violence, it remains a fact that violence itself is the deadliest of sins and the very opposite of the spirit of Our Lord.

I want in conclusion to offer you once again from the arena of the open air an experience which I think is not insignificant. I have found over thirty-four years that the average outsider expects that the Christian will be a Pacifist. He may think it is crazy. He may be quite sure it won't work. But he finds it absolutely impossible to reconcile Christianity and war. Perhaps that which most invalidates what we have to say and which most prejudices men against the kind of claims we would make, is that he sees a vital and unbridgeable chasm between the events of Good Friday which we celebrate, and the preparations of violent defence in which we are engaged—to say nothing of the panoply of violence in which most of our modern life is clothed. If it be true that when we come to the end of our Christian advocacy we appeal for a verdict and desire that those that hear us agree with us, it is just as true that such an agreement does not necessarily come in the initial stages of our preaching.

In the arena of preaching, the first step of seeking to answer the relevant questions can be successfully dealt with, even if at the end of it there is no agreement as to the decision to which we believe we must come. There is a fellowship of controversy which antedates the fellowship of agreement, and the fellowship of controversy within the realm of this arena of preaching is sufficient to give us the opportunity thereupon to proceed to a fellowship of appeal. It may sound paradoxical, but I submit to you that we need not expect that those to whom we speak will agree with the conclusions at which we arrive. All that we need expect is that they will treat the problems as seriously as we have done and will themselves realize that we have established our right to offer Christ, because in a perplexing and difficult world we have realistically faced the evils of a fallen generation and the sorrows of sin. If these things are realistically and honestly presented, we have nothing to fear from all those who profess their allegiance to Communism or to Secularism. The City of God remains.

CHAPTER IV

OPEN AIR PREACHING

Any consideration of the advocacy of the Gospel in the contemporary setting ought to give some place to a discussion of open air preaching. It is an art which should be recovered and an opportunity which we dare not lose. In one sense, Christianity was born in the open air, and the characteristic preaching of John Wesley, to say nothing of the preaching of Whitfield, was open air, field, street preaching. There is today a need for such preaching within the general framework of our advocacy and, therefore, I think it is justifiable to include it in any general survey of the contemporary scene. There are three recognizable types of open air Christian witness and they are disparate. First is the open air demonstration in the name of our Lord of which the Roman Catholics prove themselves masters in their open air celebrations of Mass, and in the great convocations out of doors with which they demonstrate the size and the fervour of their faith. Such efforts to present a shop window, so to speak, of the Christian faith are of great value. Provided they are successful they are good. Whereas the kind of demonstration which only attracts a few people may in fact cause a denigration of the Christian faith in the eyes of those who do come. Large demonstrations of the total power of the Christian Church are desperately needed, and should not be in any way condemned merely because such demonstrations are often such an integral part of more totalitarian régimes.

The open air service represents a somewhat different type of effort. From time to time we feel that we ought to take our Gospel out of doors and we make a rather pathetic effort to transfer an indoor service to the open air, expecting there the same reactions to it. If I speak with a certain amount of despair about the open air service I do so from considerable and bitter experience. A congregation singing lustily to the Lord within doors and under a roof sounds a wailing disaster out of doors. The parson who is not accustomed to open air speaking performs his office with fervour but also with a certain amount of obvious pain, and the general impact of the non-existent crowd is not to commend the Gospel but in many cases to degrade it in people's eyes. It should be considered a basic principle that unless such a meeting assumes either the size or the significance of a demonstration, it is not worth undertaking.

What I'm concerned about is the third kind of open air meeting. Its characteristics are simple to the point of bareness, and its technique and format are contained within a secular environment rather than a spiritual one. This kind of open air meeting is one upon which I've adventured myself for many years, and if I principally speak about Tower Hill, which was my first love and remains so to this day, it is not because this is itself the only type and pattern. It is because it is the one kind of open air meeting with which I have had first hand experience.

I have made some attempts to speak in the open air elsewhere with results which have not been entirely satisfactory. I ventured to Japan a couple of years ago and asked whether I could have open air meetings. They bowed deeply and said yes, and indicated that they would arrange them. They prepared an open air meeting in a place called Sapporo in Hokkaido. I felt very far from home. I felt the more remote when, thinking of Tower Hill and Hyde Park, I was escorted to the place of execution by a large gentleman with a gong, followed by two kimono-clad ladies with paper lanterns and an arbour which had been specially constructed, and inside which my interpreter and I were supposed to operate. I made my speech through the interpreter. Japanese is a language which I find it difficult to believe that anybody can speak. My interpreter, whenever I produced a sentence, produced a paragraph. This slowed up the proceedings and, finally, coming to the end of what I had to say, and feeling quite in despair, I said, through him, would anybody like to ask a question? Whereupon a little man in the front, looking extremely unlike anybody else I'd ever seen, looked up into my face and said, in perfect English, "I would like to know, Mr. Speaker, what you think the effect of Mr. T. S. Eliot's Anglo-Catholicism will be on the Church of England." I hadn't any idea, and there was not very much more that was said on that topic.

I tried to speak in Moscow. I was in Red Square and I

said to those who were shepherding me, "Can we have an open air meeting?" And they shook their heads sorrowfully and said, "No. Open air meetings are not held in Red Square." I fished out of my pocket a photograph of Lenin conducting an open air meeting in Red Square. Whereupon they said, "It's too cold." I offered to expose myself to winter's conditions for the sake of speaking. Then, of course, it was indicated to me that it was impossible to conduct open air meetings in the Red Square, and so it turned out.

I think it is true to say that apart from Sydney, New South Wales, there is no open air forum anywhere of the calibre found at Tower Hill and Hyde Park. I will venture to say a little about my own experience in these two places to indicate some of the things which I hope will not be unprofitable in a general introduction to open air preaching. It is thirty-four years ago since I first began to speak on Tower Hill—which is a kind of Mars Hill of London's dinner hour. It is the roof of a bonded warehouse and is next door to the Tower of London. To this place repair city workers, city dwellers, dock labourers, and various people whose usual avocation is in the city. For the period of the lunch hour on week-days they gather to hear all kinds of advocates of this and that. I was a very young minister and cocksure at that and I felt that I would like to say something in a wider context. This place was indicated to me. I went one Tuesday. I saw a man sitting on a wall and I said, "How do you start a meeting?" He said, "You get on the wall, Governor, and they'll come." I got up on the wall and nobody came. I said, "What do you do now?" He said, "Well, you clap your hands." I said, "Will you clap yours?" He said, "Yes." I turned to another sedentary figure and said, "Would you clap yours?" And he said, "Yes." So we had a couple of rounds of applause and the crowd gathered. I indicated that I was going to speak about religion and the crowd dispersed. But one or two remained.

Immediately, I was interrupted—somebody wanted to know what I was there for, somebody asked about Karl Marx, and we were off. It was a meeting at which there was no singing of hymns, no taking of collections, no stated prayers, no formal beginning and no formal ending. It was a free-for-all, an opportunity to communicate the Gospel within the context of question and answer. For an hour and a half each Wednesday, this process goes on.

The same is true of Hyde Park. But there are perceptible differences. Hyde Park is more of a professional occasion. There are many more women in the congregations in Hyde Park. Therefore the men tend to display themselves rather more obviously, and there is a lack of the reality which belongs to the crowd which is almost entirely masculine on Tower Hill.

It is impossible to understand the ethos or the value of an open air occasion on Tower Hill unless you reflect upon the fact that it is situated within the cockney environment. Much nonsense had been talked about the profundity of the thinking of the cockney. He's a superficial thinker, but he's a quick thinker. He is a humorous thinker. And he is a scandalous person. I mean by that that his irreverence is monumental, though I think fairly innocuous. As a case in point, I remember being suddenly confronted by a cockney who set the crowd in a roar. He wanted to know who washed up after the Last Supper. Now for you and me that may be a blasphemous, impermissible flippancy. But for the crowd which meets in an environment which has no necessary background of sanctity, such is the elementary and superficial humour with which you have constantly to contend, and no prudishness can evade it.

It is the kind of humour, not wit, which arises out of situation. Should you take your hat off somebody in the crowd will tell you to put it on quickly because the woodpeckers are about. That again is a weak joke. There is nothing of brilliance about it. Bob Hope would despise it. Nevertheless, it is part of the healthy and raw humour which characterizes this place. I have suffered many times at the hands of these natural humorists. There was one very eloquent man who came for many years. He was a cockney, a sailor, who was talking one day about alcohol, concerning which he was an expert. I said that he ought to sign the pledge. Whereat he retorted, "Didn't Paul say, 'Take a little wine for thy stomach's sake'?" I agreed that Paul did, but suggested that Paul meant "rub it in". He wouldn't accept that as the answer, so I tried to approach him on another track. I told him how dangerous it was to quote scripture and I quoted, with what I hoped to be devastating authority, the words from Proverbs, "Wine is a mocker, strong drink is raging, for at the last it biteth like a serpent and stingeth like an adder." And he said he'd been looking for that sort of stuff for the last ten years.

In that kind of spirit, the crowd will probably be prepared to accept the humour of the retort for a question which does not permit of an answer. I was once asked what shape your soul was when you died and I said "oblong". In the merriment which followed, the question was forgotten. Humorous retort has a salutary value when there is a constant interplay of irrelevant and inconsequential chatter and a very great deal of frivolity.

Anyone who seeks to offer Christ in the open air must be prepared to be as patient and, if you like, as entertaining as he can be. I recall an incident in which my sailor cockney friend received the *tu quoque*. It was when he was talking, as a professed athiest, of the impropriety of our description of the feelings of the heart. Said he, "The heart is not an instrument of feeling. The heart is a pump. That's all the heart is." I suggested that perhaps he was unmarried. He said he was. I turned to the crowd and suggested that I knew why he was unmarried. There had been an occasion when he'd fallen in love and he declared his love. He had said to his beloved, "I love you with all my pump." And she had turned him down.

Far from being totally unimportant, it is of the essence of the case to point out that there is a joyous connotation to the proclamation of the Gospel. It is in such informal occasions as open air witness that there is freer rein for the abandonment of those formalities to which we are so much addicted in church, and the opportunity, theologically as well as practically, to let our hair down. At the same time it would be quite wrong to assume that such meetings as these are entirely bereft of seriousness. The opposite is the case. Anyone who proclaims a controversial doctrine must expect ugly situations to arise. And I have not been denied such occasions. There is a particular equanimity about the average Londoner. He is, I think, politically rather more adult than most other people. There is an innate tolerance which I hope I do not misread. At the same time, if you recollect the occasions that have passed over thirty-four years, you will not be surprised to know that at the time of the great depression in 1930 there were ugly scenes. I remember on one occasion a great crowd of Communists and others paraded on Tower Hill to declare their grievances. As is the case with most demonstrations they were about an hour late, and by the time they arrived the meeting which I conducted was under way. A number of their leaders walked along the wall. I know it very well. It is about twenty-four inches wide. It has a drop of about two feet at the front and six or seven feet at the back. A number of the leaders came along and insisted that I should go home. I said I'd been there first and I had a proper right to stay where I was. They indicated that if I didn't go, they would assist me. Then a man came along carrying a banner with "Liberty" written on it, and pushed me off the wall. However, these are not the normal occasions. There is a freedom of feeling and a sudden rush of temper which evaporates as quickly, as do the mists on a sunny morning. But, there is a reality about such occasions, and reality is never far from the meeting.

I

These are the externals. What is the actual nature of the preaching? It begins in the recognition that you are there to be shot at. You are there to stand your corner, and to state your case, under conditions where you enjoy nothing of the privilege that normally you can enjoy in the dugout of the pulpit, or the escape hatch of the vestry. You are there, and while you are there you have to speak and you have to answer for the way in which you speak, as well as the content of your utterance. This is an enlightening, as well as sometimes a disabling, experience. There is nothing more ruthless than the penetrating heckling of a man who is sure that you are fumbling with words, and fundamentally unaware of·the nature of your case. There is nothing more disabling and, at the same time, more educative than to be compelled to say what you mean in language which must be as decipherable in the heat of argument as it may be elegant and suggestive when you read it at leisure.

The second and great quality that belongs to this kind of oratory, if it can be called oratory, is that the text and the subject matter are very largely decided for you. There is practically no danger that you will be talking on abstruse matters, except to yourself, for the crowd will quickly disperse if you do. You will be facing, in the light of what you believe to be the Gospel, situations which maybe you did not choose, but situations which those who listen to you regard as the substance of their case against you—or, the substance of the case which they believe you ought to profess in the name of Christ to them.

After thirty-four years I'm by no means in possession of all the answers, but I think I know most of the questions. It is of interest to recollect into what broad categories these questions fall. By far the greatest number of questions refer to the Church. That may sound strange and it may not be universally characteristic, but on the whole, I think it is general. For reasons good, bad, and indifferent, so many of those who are inclined to listen to the man who speaks to them about Jesus Christ in the open air are not prepared to listen to such a man speaking within an ecclasiastical framework. By far the greater number of them regard the Christian Church as an institution which is not equated with Christianity, and which is composed of those who have progressively departed from its spirit.

It is easy enough, and it is, in fact, the most insidious of all temptations to regard the heckler, the questioner, the sincere presenter of difficulties, as perverse in origin. It is easy enough to write him off as the product of ignorance. But it is an alarming and a continuing source of concern that this automatic assumption that Christianity has been perverted, if not betrayed, by the Church, should in fact exist.

To meet it is part of the travail of the preacher. He must hold the balance between a wholesale condemnation of the Church and a wholesale praise of it. But he will find that if he is prepared in sincerity to advocate what the Church is in spirit, and to indicate, by whatever means come to his hand, or whatever evidence he can command, that the Christian Church does possess within itself the marks of royalty and goodness as well as the marks of perversion and decay, that a response is evoked and a fellowship is established. He will probably find it impossible, within the framework of an open air meeting, to press his evangelical claims or his ecclesiastical claims beyond a certain limit. But he will be in no doubt whatsoever that the principal difficulty is to make the Church, in the eyes of those who listen, the reality which he holds it to be.

The second great area of questioning relates to the political field. In the nineteenth century Europe made the mistake of conceiving man as an economic creature. We are in danger, in the twentieth century, of conceiving man as a political animal. These are over-simplifications, yet it is unquestionable that problems of a political nature tend to predominate in public discussions. Such predominance is likely to continue for the simple reason that the general reading of the population is more and more confined to the daily press. And the daily press is almost exclusively concerned, except for the more pornographic of its details, with the political environment and with political occasions. Should the eight o'clock news bulletin contain the announcement that there was a revolution in Venezuela, that there was more shooting in Seoul, that there were a number of curious political convolutions taking place in America, you could be reasonably certain that the questions which would arise on Tower Hill would be questions about Venezuela, about Seoul and about those particular issues.

Therefore, though it is not imperative that the preacher should have any basic philosophy of life if he ventures into the open air, it is of the utmost importance that he should have read the newspaper. And perhaps the reading of the headlines of newspapers does give us a better entree to practical theology than some of the more recondite pure theologies, in which, personally, I find little contact with reality. I say this somewhat rashly perhaps. Yet it does seem to me that I have wasted a great deal of my time acquiring information about subjects which have never been mentioned in the open air, and which I feel do not belong to the ordinary and normal equipment of one who seeks to advocate Jesus Christ in those surroundings. I am quite sure that there should be some people who have learned Greek and that there should be some people who have learned Hebrew, and that there should be a great many people who have first class exegetical competence. But I have never known enough Greek to be able to pit my puny knowledge against the experts. I have less Hebrew. And I'm quite sure that if I want to find an answer to some exegetical problems I can consult a library more effectively than call upon my own scholastic reminiscences.

An essential characteristic of this kind of open air speaking is that it redresses a balance which all too dangerously has been false. It does create that sense of reality, that sense of rapport, which in many cases may otherwise never be established. If the speaker in the open air has not attended to the headlines he will be written off as an ass, and will not be listened to. And that will be his proper fate.

The third great area about which questions are propounded is the scientific. I do not share the common view that scientists are supermen. With some exceptions, I think atomic scientists are a bunch of cowards. I do not share the view that those equipped with scientific information are necessarily the best judges of spiritual matters. One of the less reputable daily newspapers in London once ran a series of articles on the next world. The first man who was asked to contribute to this series was an atheistical scientist. The assumption was that because he was an expert on some of the remoter abstractions in this world, he would be a guide to the world to come. Many a Methodist local preacher with no knowledge of the long words which proliferated in his article would have done very much better. But there is a prevailing conception, for which we are partly to blame, that it is the scientist who knows his job. Within this framework the open air preacher will be confronted with some of the most knotty problems with which he will have to deal. And the position is now very much more complicated because of space travel. I share the conviction of a very great open air preacher from the Roman Church, namely, Father Vincent McNabb, who said to me, shortly before he died, that there is nothing so perverse as the general picture modern uneducated man has acquired of the scientific cosmogony and of the general status of the man who is called a scientist. True scientists are the most humble of people, but the sordid, squalid pseudo-science, which comes to us as a kind of residual legacy of the nineteenth century's pride and arrogance, is a continuing source of embarrassment and difficulty to any preacher of the word. Unless he can acquire some working knowledge of the approach to these problems he will find himself in considerable difficulty, and will be written off by the less perspicuous of his crowd as an ignoramus.

II

There is, therefore, a preparation which is necessary for open air work. If it can be adequately set forth, perhaps many will feel that it is a proper domain and that without it one dimension of Christian advocacy must necessarily be lost. There can be little doubt that one of the predisposing impulses to open air work is a better understanding of what in fact it contains and what in fact it offers. First of all it is *sui generis*. Just as a television presentation is *sui generis*, so is the open air ministry. The failure of so many people is to assume that the technique which is appropriate to the pulpit will be appropriate to the platform on Tower Hill. Nothing is further from the truth. To maximize an emotion physically, dramatically, in a pulpit is excellent, but to maximize that facial expression in front of a television screen is calamitous. In real life the viewer watches your eyes. On a television screen the viewer watches your mouth. Just as there is a technique of television, which is very new, and very largely unlearned as yet, so there are certain distinguishable qualities about the open air which themselves are unique and yet are fairly well established.

The first is this. It is not necessary to shout your head off in order to be heard. Those who yell at the extreme intensity of their lungs are not creating a mood of attractiveness. They are repellent and they are short lived. The proper use of the voice is such that, in practice, a woman who speaks clearly can be heard much more distinctly than a man who bellows.

The essential quality is discontinuity. The crowd in the open air, unless it is particularly somnolent, is likely to be mobile, and you must catch them where they are and each sentence must contain something of note, of raciness, otherwise the development of an argument which to you may sound succinct and cogent may be too prolonged to maintain the interest of the man who passes by. Therefore, the kind of speaking which is appropriate to the open air is of the staccato variety, and the continuity of the argument matters less than the re-iteration of the truth which you seek to imply. The very simplicity of the occasion makes certain quite simple demands. You should know where to begin, but you should be prepared to be diverted at the earliest opportunity. The very stimulation of this interaction itself produces the demand from which your answer has to be made. It is thereafter a matter of being led willingly along what paths your questioner desires you to take.

The proviso is that you should use the question and not merely answer it. Very few people ask the question that is in the back of their mind. Most people ask a question which conceals the real problem. It is the genius of the master, and it is the frequent failure of the amateur, to be misled by the nature of the question. With greater perception he will be able to use that question—and using it, be able to point to the deeper issue. The man who asks about Cain's wife is asking a trivial question; but he is actually asking a question which can be turned into a whole category of answers as to the inspiration of the Bible, and as to the value of holy scripture itself.

These things can be learnt, and they are learnt according to the pattern of the immortal Dr. Spurgeon. When he was asked to preach on preaching, he delivered a sermon in which he indicated that the essence of preaching was to do it. Those who did it and continued to do it were probably those who finally became the masters at it. The temptation is to regard open air preaching as an occasional venture, the merits or demerits of which can be easily discerned after one operation. There are always those who say it is impossible to conduct open air meetings in their town. They have tried, and nobody has come. You ask them how often they've tried and they say, well the first Sunday was a bit damp, and perhaps it was understandable that no crowd came. The second Sunday was fine and warm. Still practically nobody came. We tried one more Sunday. They didn't come, so of course you can't hold open air meetings in our town. Now listen to the immortal General Booth. In a letter to my grandmother, who was remotely related to him, he said something which I have nowhere seen in print. He was advising a little group who had much trouble and little success in the East End at a particular street corner. And this is the advice he gave with his own pawky humour. "Go there each day and stand at the appointed place. Go there each day for a year, and if at the end of the year nobody has come you should reasonably consider moving around the corner."

To create the habit you have first of all to create the image. To be a lone figure talking to nobody is not the sign of disaster or of failure. It may be the necessary apprenticeship to a condition which later may prevail, in which those who come will come in fair weather or foul. In thirty-four years on Tower Hill we've only been prevented from holding the meeting on six occasions. It is an impressive testimony to those who are accustomed to a particular pattern of church attendance that so many would rather brave a wintry day than lose the opportunity of the excitement and the fun.

III

There are perceptible and recognized limitations to such a ministry. In fact it is a pro-ministry or a pre-ministry. It is ridiculous to assume that all the spiritual and ecclesiastical accoutrements of a church can attach to an open air meeting. The man who says how many converts did you get last week is linguistically at fault and certainly has no real and valid case behind his question. What happens in the open air is that you provide a shop window for the case you want to present. You break down some of the barriers whereby it is less difficult for those who hear you, if you are convincing and sincere, to take other steps which elsewhere will be offered. But to present the full Gospel in the glare, the humour, the tension, and the inconsequence of an open air meeting is to ask the impossible. Many a time it has been my lot to spend an hour and a quarter fiddling about with this and that—getting into wrangles and out of them—debating the inequities of politicians and suffering the attacks upon the Church, for the sake, in the last two or three minutes, of advocating Christ.

Because, as a Methodist, I believe that personal testimony here is worth a peck of suggestion and precept, I would like to tell you of the way in which the meeting ended on a Wednesday in Holy Week on Tower Hill. It was a cold day. There was one other man trying to collect a crowd. He was of fundamentalist persuasion and his audience was very small. I was addressing the main body of the crowd and we were talking about Apartheid, we were talking about nuclear disarmament, and strangely, for no reason at all, we were talking about bi-metallism. And among the other topics there was the question about NATO, there was a question about Nasser. It was only after I'd been going for almost ninety minutes that the opportunity came. I seized it as best I could and told them of Good Friday. Had I begun by saying something about the Saviour upon the cross, had I then attempted to declare my own faith in His redeeming love, had I then invited them to stand beneath that cross, had I then sought to tell them of the love of Christ, I should not have been able to speak to their real needs. I should not have been able in fact to arrest their attention. But because I had endeavoured, as patiently as I could, to face these other questions with an innate sense of fairness, they felt it was only right and proper that they should give me the chance at the end of saying what I had to say.

And the supreme reward of open air speaking is that from time to time out of the murky sky of debate, out of the dangerous pools of humour, out of the occasional tensions of hatred and malice, there come these golden moments when that for which we most yearn becomes gloriously possible. To seize those moments, not asking for any reward, save that of knowing we do His will, to declare one's own faith, to commend one's own Lord, and to say to those who never darken the doors of the church something about the cross of Christ, is sheer and unlimited joy, and is a reward of priceless worth. I can remember how the words of that meeting concluded and I will repeat them to you. I spoke of Jesus upon the cross. The crowd was silent. One man wanted to interrupt and somebody told him to shut up. He shut up. And I was able to go on and I finally said, "And I believe, my friends, that there is life in a look at the crucified One." That was my reward, and I believe by God's grace, a not unworthy fulfilment of a piece of my ministry.

CHAPTER V

EVANGELISTIC PREACHING

IF we have the heart of the matter within us as preachers, and if we yearn for the salvation of the world, then for us all preaching is substantially evangelistic. That is to say, all preaching must be concerned so to press the claim as to evoke a verdict. Unless the verdict is expected, then the process of preaching would be largely nullified. But there lies the problem as well as the opportunity. For we are confronted with a situation in which evangelistic preaching has become narrowed to certain configurations of thought and expressions of theological bent, and has become associated with certain reactions not all of them as commendable as they are vociferously championed.

It would be perhaps not unsuitable for us to consider in the first instance some of those demurrers which are offered by sensible people, and sometimes by not so sensible people, to the claims of evangelistic preaching, and thereby to remind ourselves of the diffidence with which some of us might care to have the word "evangelism" attached to our own proclamation of the Gospel. One of the supreme problems seems to be that a great proportion of evangelistic fervour today is expended without due regard for the sanctity and the value of personality. We ask too much and we ask it too soon. We tend to impose ourselves upon our audiences or our congregations without due care to respect their personalities and without due care to play fair in our speaking. There is something that is *prima facie* undesirable in the attempt to jockey any human being into a premature decision for which the grounds have not been sufficiently declared. This indecent haste, with which we seek a verdict, incapacitates evangelism at the very point where it would be at its richest and most potent. Furthermore, inasmuch as it is hasty, there is not sufficient time for the deploying of suitable argument, and compensation is found in the emotional realm for a lack of reality, or of consistency, or, indeed, of preparation in the intellectual realm. It is not true, of course, that to "roll them in the aisles" is necessarily either the function or the achievement of the evangelist today. But it is true that the emotional superstructure of such evangelism is proportionately very much greater than the weight of argument upon which it is reared.

In the third place, there is no obvious and irrefutable evidence that the results of such evangelical efforts are effective in creating a higher quality of human life. In fact, there is a kind of repetitive evangelism which at best keeps people on a level. Every practising minister knows that there are some people in his congregation who are addicted to conversion and find it a suitable and a periodic process, very often round about Easter time. They are none the worse for it, but a perceptive onlooker would not see any appreciable difference in their lives represented by the number of conversions to which they have subjected themselves.

Furthermore, and this is perhaps the most disabling of all the characteristics of much evangelism today, it predisposes the recipient or the sufferer to a kind of permanent infantilism. He finds himself in the cradle where it is warm and comfortable. The offer of Christ is made without due emphasis on the responsibilities which follow, and very often the experience is regarded as an end in itself. Consequently there is a predisposition on the part of the recipient of these blessings to cherish them in circumstances in which they will not be snatched from him—and finding the warmth and security of the cradle, he seeks it as a permanent spiritual home. He never learns to use his legs and never develops his spine. From the day of his first conversion to the last stages of his progress, he remains in lively and repeated expectation of a repetition of the early experiences which he first enjoyed. He finds a sense of comfort and assurance in the fact that the cradle exposes him to practically none of the strong tides of passion or the stronger demands of morality.

Once again these strictures may appear to be unnecessarily strong. If an academic assessment were to be made of the results of evangelism it could be, of course, shown that some of the greatest Christians have passed through this process and, far from being the worse for it, have, in fact, become redeemed and transformed and can look to the process as the beginning of a long and glorious journey. At the same time, it could be true to say that the appreciable results of the various evangelical episodes in the Christian life over the last 100 years have not been accompanied by any perceptible and dynamic increase in the moral tone of those who have undergone them. It would be impossible to point to any perceptible development in the moral character of the people among whom I live as a result of the quite astronomical effects at the time of the ministries of American evangelists. That is not to say, and I should be the last to attempt to say it, that good results did not flow. It is to say that if evangelism is to be limited to the characteristics and results to which I have now given some time, then it cannot be the universal occupation of the Christian ministry. It is at best one of the methods to which a preacher must direct himself, and even then to a limited congregation and sparingly and not as the normal or a complete expression of his ministry.

I hope that I have said this with sufficient care because, as we say these things even to ourselves, if we are concerned with the faith which we seek to profess, then it becomes increasingly obvious to us that the alternative to the evangelism which we asperse is a deeper and fuller evangelism to which we have not yet sufficiently given either our hearts or our minds. It is to that wider evangelism, therefore, that I would invite you to address your thoughts now.

From the human standpoint—that is from the standpoint of the preacher as he preaches and the hearer who receives what he has to say—a certain guiding and ultimate principle seems to me immediately to emerge from any endeavour to discover what is the objective in evangelical preaching. The objective surely is to evoke a response of the will; for we cannot determine an experience. Shortly speaking Christianity, in my estimation, is ninety-five per cent obedience. The superstructure of emotional reaction, the assurance which sometimes accompanies the processes of righteousness, but not necessarily so, cannot be commanded. We ought to fight very shy of feeling. For to be satisfied with conversion, if it produces a certain process of feeling in those who are converted, is a shoddy and totally inadequate kind of conversion—if, indeed, it is worthy of such a title at all.

Our true Protestant tradition would aver that the essence of our appeal must be to the will, garnished by suitable emotional accompaniments or reactions, and expressed in a suitably intellectual or, at least, intelligible form. Those who respond must not expect to see a bright light which will irradiate their path—though they will be blessed if such a light comes to lighten their darkness. They must not expect to hear an authentic voice which will once and for all dispose of their doubts—though they should be grateful for any dispersement of such doubts. They must be content to make a response of the will and thereafter to trust and to obey. Such a hard and rigorous faith is the one faith that can stand supreme and unchallenged in the kind of world in which we preach for conversion and decision in this twentieth century.

But that is only a part of the problem. For the rest it is a question of total response, which in most cases is an improper claim to make and cannot be the prelude to an appropriate and final response on the part of the hearer.

For it seems beyond question that what we are facing as preachers is a varied state of mind in our hearers, from whom we are only entitled to expect the kind of response which at that time they are capable of making. The true evangelistic preaching of our time must be a preaching which gears the claims it makes on the wills of its hearers to the particular state wherein those hearers are to be found. There are stages of response which can be expected from preaching to the pagan, preaching to the porch, preaching to the pew, and preaching to the penitent-form. I hope this alliteration is more than artful. These differentiations distinguish clearly marked conditions, and must be recognized as the determinants of the kind of response we expect and are entitled to expect.

I

In England not so very long ago a survey was taken to discover the religious state of the people. In two sample areas answers were sought to certain quite positive and definite questions. The report is a quite devastating document. It was found that only ten per cent of the people go to church; and many of those who don't go to church have forgotten the name of the church they stay away from. Most people perhaps go to church at least three times, but on two of those occasions they are relatively unconscious, and on the third occasion they're quite unconscious so perhaps they can't count for the record.

Now the serious substance of this particular document lies in the fact that there is a growing community which does not remember the Songs of Zion learnt at mother's knee, which cannot recite the Lord's Prayer, and which has no nostalgia for religion whatsoever. These are the true pagans, in the accepted and classical sense of that word. These are the people to whom a particular kind of evangelism is proper and all other kinds of evangelism are improper. These are the people, and there are increasing numbers of them in the predominately secular world in which we live, for whom evangelical preaching, if it is to be effective at all, must begin from the beginning and make no assumptions whatsoever. Every evangelical episode in the last fifty years in England has almost totally failed to make any impact upon this growing community of the real outsider. It obviously demands a radical approach, and much of that approach must be done in completely secular surroundings.

It has been at this point that some of us have been working, for over twenty years now, in the Order of Christian Witness. We have found, for one thing, that group work is essential. The man who is not prepared to stand on a chair at a street corner and talk to a bunch of miners may, under due pressure and sustenance from a group in which he has prepared himself, find the necessary strength to do it and, what is more, the necessary zest to do it again. It is in the fellowship of creative evangelical effort to pagans that I believe there is to be discovered a power of evangelism which is not to be discovered by the single minister or the single advocate.

The Order of Christian Witness operates in the following way. We select a town to which we would like to go and then we extract an invitation from them to go. We facilitate that invitation by saying that we will pay for ourselves. We will ask no fee, which gives us liberty in preaching, and gives our hosts a chance of saying, if they dislike us, that they have no particular financial responsibility for what we've been doing. We require of those who are prepared to go with us that they should pay the full fare and their full board, and we offer them in return the floors of schoolrooms and a palliasse of straw and the opportunity of paying for their own food. What we then insist upon is that the group should train itself in the practice of fellowship, a word which is never of any use unless you attach an economic as well as a spiritual interpretation to it. But the real essence of that fellowship is the living together of those who are seeking to make an evangelical approach out of their own community to the pagan who is quite outside the Church. There is a precious and unique quality about the fellowship which comes, as anyone who has experienced the joys of camping knows, from living together.

And then this community, living together and paying together, putting in what it can and taking from the common fund what it needs, sets about the task of preparing itself. Each member of the community is required to prepare a five-minute address on any topic he likes— provided it is a topic upon which he has some authority to speak. Usually it is a topic that begins in personal experience and ends in a witness to the love of God within that experience. When they have prepared this five-minute speech, they submit it to their friends, who cut out all the irrelevant and unnecessary words and its authors then have three minutes to make up. They go back and they write it out again. It is astonishing the number of words that can be quite properly extracted like useless and carious teeth. Discarding words affords the opportunity for the kind of preparation which is absolutely imperative, a preparation in which what is said shall be simple, understandable and shall not overstep the mark of five minutes. Then we have the opportunity of speaking in canteens and at street corners. And one by one the volunteers do it.

What is the evangelical response that we then ask? It is that those who are interested in what we say should be prepared to come back with us and taste something of the fellowship from which the utterance, the message, the witness was made. And, though it may sound almost a confession of defeat, I believe that to the pagan, the real outsider, anything but a sustained and continuous process of evangelism that proceeds through all the stages I have indicated, anything but that, must be content with not much expectation of response. If it be of any comfort, we have found that those who are prepared to listen to what we have to say, to catch some note of sincerity and of relevance in what is said, and thereafter to get to know the fellowship of the Order of Christian Witness, have made the sort of response which God will accept and bless in their lives as the first step towards His Kingdom.

II

The second group is not totally remote from the Church, but has memories of churchmanship, probably nostalgic; those who will attend church perhaps on Easter Day or Christmas Day but are not likely to come at any other time. There are many retired colonels in England who would never dream of attending church normally to hear that most revolutionary document, the Magnificat, but will, on Easter Day and on Christmas Day, with deep sincerity attend church. They are the people who can properly be designated as belonging to the porch. They do not belong to the pew, and are certainly not to be found within the holy of holies. What is to be done with them? What kind of approach can be made?

They fall into certain quite obvious categories.

There is, first, the category of youth. The youth club. There is secondly the category of the occasional visitor or the occasional adherent. And there is the ever-enlarging category of those who once-upon-a-time went to church, and once-upon-a-time were probably officers in the church, but have drifted away and now have not come at all for many years. There is a literature about evangelical preaching to this group. There have been endeavours to marry the rhythm of Fats Waller to the processes of evangelism, to explore the possibilities of folk mass in basic jazz and to indicate the crying need for the kind of service which can influence them when they do come. Indeed, an important part of the problem here, though not the entire problem, is to stimulate a renewed desire for church going. This witness to the erstwhile churchgoer involves some pretty radical thinking about the conduct of our services of worship.

I remember some years ago being invited to take part in an evening service at a well-known central hall in the south-west of England. In the vestry I was given what they described as the programme, and indeed it was. There was a long introit, there was a sung Lord's Prayer, there was a long anthem, not appropriate as far as I remember, two solos, three chorus hymns, two other hymns and a Benediction, also sung. I was told that the sermon ought to be short because the buses went at about 7.30, and if people missed the buses it would delay their return home. That is the sort of thing from which we suffer. It was a programme, at best a sacred concert, at worst an orgy of loud singing of ill-considered hymnology. There was only one opportunity for prayer on the programme, and that was at the early part of the service. There was an expectation of much jollity, and I've no doubt that a great many people were hoping for a good time.

Now such exercises have disqualifications but the principal disqualification is this: worship cannot be participation by sitting down and appreciating, even at its best, what somebody else is doing. The essence of the preaching in the porch is to evoke a response from those who are at present unprepared to take any radical part in churchmanship—to evoke a response from them at the point of liturgy, if it is impossible at this moment to expect a response at the point of decision in moral matters.

But the liturgy was never intended under God to be an occasion for the presentation of tuneful numbers and suitable responses made by choirs at the minister's invitation. They were intended to be the full participation of a congregation and minister and choir, for that matter, in the exercise of dramatic and vital worship of God.

We now know as never before what constituted the very earliest services of the Christian Church. One of the great deliverances of scholarship of our present age is that there is no longer a scintilla of doubt as to the way in which the first Christians worshipped. They obviously did not worship in ecclesiastical buildings. There were none. They worshipped in houses, which meant that they worshipped in a room, for most houses had but one room. We know that the table, normally in the middle of the room or near the middle of the room, was put on the Gradus. Indeed, in the mass today, the Psalm which is interspersed between the Epistle and the Gospel is still called the Gradual, not on account of the pace at which it is taken, but because it was first performed on the Gradus—the raised part of the floor. We know that those early services were a dramatic re-presentation, re-enactment of the Passion of Our Lord, of which the supreme point, of course, was the Communion Service, the Eucharistic prayer, what our friends in Rome call the mass and what our friends in Moscow call the liturgy. This is now beyond dispute. I believe that very largely the efficacy of their early preaching was contained in the participation evoked from the worshippers. Many of them, coming from Judaism, were not prepared to enter into a full understanding of the claims of the cross, but were drawn into the panoply, the beauty, and the activity of church worship.

We have with this group the opportunity of presenting our evangelism in a clear-cut invitation to respond to the challenge of church, and to participate in the actual expressions of churchmanship.

III

Now to that third group, those who are hardened churchgoers or, at least, the regular churchgoers. Those who are prepared to worship on Sunday provided you ask nothing more of them for the rest of the day; those who are as ardent and as temporary in their devotions as can reasonably be expected; those who, in fact, constitute perhaps the main body of the listening public to the message of the Gospel. What is the kind of evocation that we can properly express and demand here? It is, I believe, a moral one. These people, before they can come to the mystical experience of conversion in its fullest sense, must go through the process of a response to the moral demands of the Christian faith. The great and outstanding difference between the evangelism of our day and the evangelism of Moody and Sankey was that there was then a far greater emphasis upon certain simple moral demands. You laid off the drink, you stayed away from the horses, you retained a view of the marriage vow which was simple, narrow, and pure.

You kept yourself unspotted from the world. You were required to pay your debts faithfully and regularly, and to offer an example of a life which was without blemish.

Now if a preacher as his evangelical claim makes this demand for moral righteousness, two things will happen. If he suitably frames his appeal he can expect a response from people who will say, "Yes, I am prepared to try to do that." And he will find that those who make that effort will fail.

It is when people who come to church with some sense of seriousness are challenged with the clear demands of the Christian faith, that a feeling of sin and guilt will appear. Such demands were always present in the evangelism of other days but unfortunately are by no means always present in evangelism today. What we can say to the hardened churchgoer is something like this: "If you will not be ashamed of yourself because of your personal delinquencies then be ashamed of the fact that you belong to a community which enjoys prosperity while so many of your fellows live in poverty and squalor. If you will not accept your own personal responsibility for the evil, shall we say, of intemperance, then will you at least look at the ravages of alcoholism and will you at least look at the effects that are produced upon little children. If you will not accept your own personal sense of sin, then will you at least be open to the argument that it is as wicked for a motorist to occupy somebody else's territory on the road as it is for a burglar to occupy somebody else's territory in a house." Here are the expressions of the moral obligation—the moral imperative of the Christian case.

What happens? Those who accept them, those who make some immediate if tentative response to them, are confronted with the basic fact which is included in the whole of our contemporary and apostolic theology, that man is a fallen creature and he is saved, if he is saved at all, not by his own efforts, but by grace which is the gift of God.

Now it is at that point that the impact and the energy of evangelical preaching can be transformed from an appeal to certain statistical and carefully designed responses, and can be made an appeal for total surrender. For the sense of guilt is reborn when men have battled sincerely with their ideals and have found their intentions have let them down, when men have confronted certain moral objectives, and have found they haven't the power or the consistency to reach them.

IV

And so we come in the last context to the preaching at the penitent form. Much of this preaching has been extracted from, subtracted from, divorced from its proper and true environment. It is the failure of evangelical evangelism that the appeal has been isolated from the disciplined framework of that practical dramatic enactment of the passion of Christ which was its proper home and in which it found its true dynamic. It is a tragedy that we invite people to commit their lives entirely to

God and then leave them stranded upon a more or less uninhabited island. The man who has been converted is but a child born into a new environment. He needs the leading strings of discipline, as he needs the comfort of love. Above all, he needs to be put to school in Christ. The man whose response is made at the point where he is ready to make it, out of a sense of guilt, out of a sense of frustration, must be set within the tutelage of a whole pattern of Eucharistic worship.

I am not a sacerdotalist. I do not claim that the Order of Communion as set out in South India is either better, or worse, than the Order of Communion as set out in the simpler forms of other communions. I make no special plea for any particular order. Coming to these matters comparatively late in life, I was sadly uninstructed in them. But I have found there is a large body of agreement in them all. In Moscow I was a member of a religious delegation. It was somewhat hastily assumed that we would like to spend our time in religious exercises, and we were taken from cathedral to cathedral. Each cathedral service lasted three hours, and there was nowhere to sit. The cathedrals were crowded with worshippers. I remember the strangeness of them—the walls plastered, or adorned, with icons; the worshippers, sometimes responding to the thunderous words and monotonous sounds of the deacon, some of them prostrating themselves, some with tears in their eyes, little children gaily bouncing up and down, old people with all the world of misery or hope looking at an icon, crossing themselves. It all seemed so strange until somebody put into my hand a copy of the liturgy that was going forward. And I found that, with some perceptible changes and what I would regard as perversions, the liturgy was substantially the Communion Service.

It is an increasing conviction of my own that, in whatever form the Communion Service is set forth, and whatever may be the particular significance we attach to it—either recollection, or remembrance, or sacrifice, or sacrament—these things although they are important are not finally decisive. What is decisive is that when those to whom we appeal have come to that point at which they can make a total response, then that total response should be made within the framework, the pattern, the ideology, the mysticism, the meaning, and all the imagery of the self-giving of Christ, the offering of Christ, the *Totus Christus*.

There is a magnificent discipline about the service. Many years ago a man on Tower Hill in a moment of expansiveness said to me, "I like the Communion Service because in it you have the whole of Christianity in twenty-five minutes." Now he was perhaps a little impatient, and he was not putting the matter with theological precision. But he was saying something which was exactly true. If we are to present Christ, and ask that those who receive what we have to say will make a response of their personalities as a whole and will give themselves to Christ, then we are only entitled to make that request within the due preparation of synaxis, the pro-communion, the pre-communion, the setting out of the claims, the recognition of our sin, the offer of Christ, the preparedness to give what we have, and the recognition that we could give no more. We hear the comfortable words "Come unto Me, all ye that labour and are heavy laden, and I will give you rest." And then we come in obedience to receive what He has to offer. There are comparatively few things that our blessed Lord tells us to do, because he is well aware that we couldn't do them anyhow. He doesn't tell us to be good. The Beatitudes aren't instructions in piety. He doesn't tell us to get rid of our doubts, because he knows that we cannot. But what he does say is, "Do this, in remembrance of Me." And there is the heart and the substance of true evangelical preaching.

Whether or not we have a right to expect the kind of results which we would crave to see is not ultimately ours to decide. It is ours to decide whether we will take the trouble so to present our evangelical claims to those who hear us that we shall ask only those things which we are entitled to ask with full respect for their personality and in view of their condition. That we should be content with any of the preliminary stages in evangelism I have treated would be sacrilegious; but we should with great care reserve our evangelism, in its total application, to such a surrounding and situation as will give it time and place, significance and purpose, and the proper discipline which is objective and not subjective. Only if we do these things will our evangelism be acceptable to God and be fruitful. Whenever I think of these matters I remember the invitation contained in the Book of Common Prayer. It is the best introduction to evangelical preaching, and to the claim that we put upon those who hear us that they should give themselves in faith and in penitence to the Redeeming Lord.

"Ye therefore who truly and earnestly repent of your sins, and are in love and charity with your neighbours, and intend to lead a new life, following the Commandments of God, and walking from henceforth in His holy ways, draw near with faith, and take this holy Sacrament to your comfort."

CHAPTER VI

THE PROSPECTS OF PREACHING

MARK TWAIN is reported to have said that when he was a boy of fifteen he was appalled at the ignorance of his father, but when he became a man of twenty-one he was gratified to discover how much the old man had picked up in the meantime. There is a wise caution in that which we should remember when peering into the future. For when the future comes we shall be part of it. There is something irrational in endeavouring to speculate upon a future from the standpoint of a rigid and unyielding present, because we are so much the creatures of immediacy. And sufficient unto the day is the evil thereof. Our main business is to concern ourselves with serving God as best we may in preaching now, and then to await with some confidence and tranquillity the days that lie ahead.

Yet a responsibility lies upon preachers to endeavour to exercise something of the prophetic function as well as the priestly one. They may shy away from it for a number of very sound and reputable reasons. Along with sound and reputable reasons there are others also, not so reputable or so sound. For example, there is a disposition in many quarters today to regard the prospects of preaching generally as dim, and therefore to be concerned not so much with future prospects as with the efforts at the moment to stave off an evil day which is felt to be well-nigh inevitable.

The attempt to anticipate the prospects of preaching may only clarify a situation which dimly as yet we recognize to be forbidding. And yet, whatever the demurrers and dangers, there is unquestionably a ministry of the word as well as of the sacraments; and whatever may be the prospects which invite us or which would deter us to preach, the sacrament of words is part of the inalienable responsibility of the servants of God. Whatever form preaching may take in the dim or the approximate future, we are committed to it, by the grace of God, as an essential part of our ministry.

What, then, are some of the prospects which may await us? What are the difficulties they present and the challenges which are represented by them?

I

There is, for one thing, the problem of our authority. There is a growing tendency for preaching today to achieve effectiveness by becoming fundamentalist, or obscurantist. This is an expression in the spiritual realm of that same totalitarianism which, in material and political forms, has long since grieved us, and from which, mercifully, some of us have been temporarily and, I hope, permanently relieved.

My own visits to the mission field have acquainted me, all too unfortunately, with the kind of effectiveness which belongs to this form of preaching, and the kind of gloss which it invariably implies in the total life of the Christian community. We are likely to see the process increase before it declines. Such preaching speaks to the immediate needs of the modern world as a result of the sins of our fathers, but it is something to which we must give an emphatic NO, and against which finally we must mobilize our resources because it is intellectually disreputable and ultimately it will prove morally negligible.

There can be little doubt that the transfer of the sense of absolute authority from a papacy to a book has been intellectually calamitous. If today any kind of totalitarianism in religion is to succeed, it will be more likely to do so when grounded in a papal theory of infallibility than in a sense of the indefectible quality of Scripture. It is possible to maintain the doctrine of infallibility by the simple process of not saying anything. The doctrine may cause exasperation in practical affairs. How much I wish his Holiness of Rome would at this moment declare that there is no such thing as a just war, as he must, of course, know. But, in fact it is a preferable type of authority, though it is, I believe, one that has to be rejected.

The effort to transfer infallibility to a library of books results in the kind of totalitarian advocacy which begins with the proposition "the Bible says". We know that the Bible says anything you would like it to say provided you look for a text to support your own egregious opinions. That is not cynicism, but an obvious fact. I was once addressing some Divinity students of fundamentalist leanings. Having finished what I had to say I was challenged on this very point of Biblical infallibility, or the total inspiration of the Bible. I ventured to ask those who were handling their Bibles, almost with ferocity at that point, whether or not they could tell me who carried the cross. They seemed to think that they could, and began to set about the necessary research. I asked them, before they began, where they were likely to find it and what they were likely to discover when they did find it. They said that Jesus carried the cross until he was exhausted, then Simon of Cyrene carried it the rest of the way to Calvary and the Bible said so. Then they proceeded to try to find the evidence. Of course they didn't because it isn't there. What is recorded in the Bible is a dual version. The Synoptic Gospels say that Simon of Cyrene carried the cross; John says that Jesus carried the cross. Nowhere is it said that the carrying of the cross was divided between our exhausted Lord and the stranger from the country. This was a very low church Protestant College. And when I finally told them that this was Church tradition coming from the stations of the cross, they felt extremely sorry about it. They felt that somebody had let them down. And that was a perfectly proper reaction—somebody had let them down. Sooner or later this totalitarian view of the Bible will impair, if not completely destroy in intelligent minds, the relationship between truth and faith. In generosity of spirit we must resolutely declare that Biblical infallibility is not part of the deposit of the Eternal Faith. It is incompatible with honesty and must be rejected.

Now, many who have already made such a rejection, have found themselves in a position which is, to use the economic word, no longer viable. For once you deny the infallibility of the Bible, any other concept of its inspiration is theologically worthless. It is possible to assert a total position of authority. It is never possible to communicate and assert a partial view of authority.

A modern writer has put the case with great persuasiveness. Reread Shaw's *Saint Joan.* Shaw perceived and stated with arresting eloquence the truth, that the inner voice may be authentic but it can never be ultimately communicated to others. That is our problem.

We may hope that out of ecumenicity will come a revival of the true sense of the general council of the Church. It may well be that the Christian Churches are moving toward such a desired haven, not of absolute authority but of possible agreement and of the growing sense of the witness of Christ; if not of objective certainty at least of subjective certitude.

This is no easy matter upon which even to speak. But, sooner or later, we must say of fundamentalist authoritarianism that it is unchristian and cannot be reconciled with the spirit of Jesus. Otherwise our mistaken charity will lead us into the jaws of final fissiparous Christian organization, and will in no way defend us from that growing attack which is made upon the Christian Church. This is the charge to which I have previously referred. We are saying things for the good of people's souls which, on reputable evidence, can be seen to be untrue. That is one of the prospects of preaching which haunts me. It is one of the prospects of preaching which if unremedied by our fervour and our intelligence, may well continue to disable us.

As a footnote to this, it is impossible to work out a doctrine of social righteousness from a position of totalitarianism. That was as obvious in Nazi Germany as it is obvious in the Protestant sects. Whatever the sincerity with which it is advocated, totalitarianism is rooted in error, is ultimately heresy, and must so be regarded and dismissed.

II

There is another theme to be explored in the same general category. It is a sardonic comment on our modern world that the more they dig for oil in the Middle East, the more are they likely to dig up scrolls which help us, either to understand, or further to be in doubt about, the original documents of the Christian religion. I remember the fun and games that took place in public arenas like Tower Hill when the first Dead Sea Scrolls were brought to light. Since then there have been many who have leapt to the defence of the Christian faith and have pointed out that the teacher of righteousness must not be confused with Jesus of Nazareth.

Whatever may be the particular and scholarly deliverances of these scrolls, it is the surrounding suggestions and the involvement of the Christian Church in a new situation which holds out for us another embarrassing and, perhaps, a challenging problem. For centuries it was more or less assumed, with minor differences of opinion, that we knew the sum total of available evidence, papyrus and document, which enabled us to build up a reasonable picture of the way in which the

Christian religion began—the historicity of the Christian faith. Now a situation has arisen in which once again the matter is wide open. There are so many things now which can be held to be in dispute and about which the careful scholar will say we must await further evidence. This continuous process of adding to or eroding upon the deposit of historicity is one which does not in detail distress the hearer who is likely to attend to the words of the average preacher next Sunday. But it does create a blanket, or general mistiness, of doubt, which is likely to increase. I am afraid lest we take it all too easily.

The new situation may have some interesting implications for those whose Christianity is focused upon the adoration of the Blessed Virgin Mary. Clearly this does not derive from the New Testament, with its suggestion of the estrangement of our Lord from His mother, but derives from the content of early Christian practice and the growth of early Christian belief. This again is unsupported by the kind of evidence upon which we rear our suppositions about the teaching of our Lord. But it seems at least possible that documents may be discovered which will lend colour either to the New Testament impression, or to the position taken by our friends of Rome. How then will we re-assert our faith in the historicity to which we have always doffed our hats, but historicity which is still not something taken irrefragably and entirely out of a past, as the mammoth, which I saw in Moscow, was taken out of the snows of Siberia, eternally preserved in its pristine form?

We are now in a position of fluidity, not only in the

realm of liturgy, not only in the realm of the development of Christian ethical standards or the application of those standards to contemporary situations. We may be on the edge of an entirely new revelation from the past about the historical circumstances which surround and condition our ultimate faith. The question which arises for us as preachers is how to open our minds, and how to prepare ourselves, so that when such eventualities do arise, if they do, we shall be not transfixed with horror, or stampeded with fury, or paralysed with ignorance, but enabled to see that truth is of God and any addition to the truth can only glorify the essence of the faith to which we are committed.

III

There is a third area in which tremendous changes are occurring. It is, broadly, the area of scientific research, particularly as it is directed toward outer space. The subject is cluttered up with the absurdities of space fiction and a great deal of nonsense is talked about it, but nevertheless it represents a new field of human interest and awareness. I was listening some time ago to a well-known British scientist who was describing outer space. I sat with great interest and heard his introduction. He said to me and to seven or eight million other people, "I want to try and tell you something about the relationship of the world in which you live to the universe around you. I want you to imagine an entirely empty London Bridge Station." I thought that was a very pleasant thing to think about. I thought of an absolutely empty

London Bridge Station. And then he said, "I want you to imagine a speck of dust somewhere near one of the exits." So I imagined a speck of dust somewhere near one of the exits. And he said, "That is the sort of relationship which the planet on which we live bears to the particular universe in which we live, our particular galactic system, which in its turn is on the edge of an even larger and emptier London Bridge Station."

What the statement conveys is something far more significant than the actual words in which it is put. It involves an attitude to the universe as something not only spatially different and enormous but qualitatively enormous and different. Professor Lovell, who is an outstanding British physicist, says that it is now at least conceivable for human beings to enter outer space and remain there, at a sufficient distance from the earth, for ten years, and then to return to the earth if they can; and if they can, they will find that ten thousand years have elapsed since they've been away. Now you and I cannot entertain that as a thought. We can understand the words but we boggle at the prospect. We can say to ourselves, "How remarkable!" or "How absurd!" or "How cozy!", but what we cannot do is so to think ourselves outside our concepts of time and space. Nevertheless there is likely to be a considerable and growing impression among ordinary people that what we regard as the uniqueness of Divine Revelation is a local, temporary affair, confined to a more or less fugitive planet, part of a very small world, in which the concept of time and space may also be local, fitting into a developing

concept of the universe, which with each new radio tele-
scope becomes more bewildering, more shattering, but at
the same time more exciting.

Now I have heard many attempts on the part of fervent
Christians, and intelligent ones, to offset this problem
by saying, "Well you don't deal with quality by merely
describing quantity." And there are many things in the
New Testament which are timeless, nor is the offer of
Christ confined to any one time or position or place.
It nevertheless remains true that with the first visitor
from outer space—and for all I know they are here now
—who makes himself not only cognizant but friendly,
we shall be confronted with a world so vastly different
from the world in which hitherto we have lived as to
astound us, as it already astounds and at the same time
attracts the true scientist.

It is not only in those things which are infinitely large
that this problem exists. It exists also in the realm of
those things which are infinitely small. It seems to me so
important that we Christian people shall not be saying
on Wednesday what the intelligent scientists have been
trying to say on the previous Monday—that we shall not
be the backers-up or the backers-out of problems which
are, at the moment, being solved elsewhere. There is no
place for Christian preaching except in the forefront of
life. And to be the adjutants, the aides-de-camp, the
junior partners of a scientific philosophy or ideology is
not only an insult to our Lord, it is an impossible position
in which to find ourselves.

Now in this smaller realm it is conceivable that within

the next few years it may be possible at least to contemplate physical immortality, or, shall we say, earthly immortality. Those who know most about it are not very far from the processes which, when they have understood them more fully, will enable men to govern metabolism, anabolism, and decay. What impresses me is not the arrogance of those who talk about immortality in time. It is the calm assurance with which they are laying plans for such eventualities. We know that the pace of change and the probability of violent or vast change has been accelerated in the last two hundred years, and has been doubly accelerated in the last fifty years. Though it may be true to say that men will always need to be told how to conquer their sins, how to overcome their lusts, how to make their peace with their neighbours, and how to live with themselves, yet here are numerous problems which will confront the preaching of the future. The criticism is often made that we as Christian people are irrelevant in what we have to say and are out of date in what we have to offer. Although we cannot obviously make long and protracted studies in the new fields, we must take them into account if we are to present an acceptable Gospel to our hearers, and to make that acceptable Gospel consonant with the faith which we profess.

IV

How shall we meet the future of preaching, filled as it is with so many new problems?

We shall need a new charity of mind, in which we are

less anxious to say in precise words what we believe, and more anxious to do in dramatic fashion what we believe to be a representation of eternity. All that is included in what has been said about sacramental worship. It is re-inforced by the conviction which the linguistic philo-sophers have forced upon us, that our words can so often cloak the true meaning of our thoughts, and that in any case we talk too much. The attempt to reduce the con-fusion of life to neat and tidy aphorisms, to be content when we see a recognizable word, and only to be satis-fied when we can agree to sign along a dotted line to a number of abstract statements, will be a decreasingly viable proposition for the Christian Church. It will be in another sphere, the sphere of practical loyalty to that all-embracing presentation by Christianity of the picture of ultimate reality, that the answer will lie, a picture which we have so distorted, and a picture which in so many respects we have ignored. We are, as Protestants, quite willing to serve God with the beautiful sounds that attract us and come to our ears from organs well played in churches. We are astonished when anybody suggests that incense would be appropriate in a Protestant church; but I have never been satisfied that if you can love God with a good sound, you dare not approach him with a good smell. Furthermore, the wealth of our approach to God in this practical way will be found as rewarding as our fathers found the concordance of doctrinal state-ment.

As a further practical assertion on this theme, I believe that the hope of the world is to marry the faith of the

West to those new discoveries of community good that are emerging in the East. In many respects the contemporary situation conforms to the pattern of that simple illustration of our Lord, who talked of two brothers and the father who said to one of them, "Go and work in my vineyard," and the son said, "Of course I will, father, I am your son and I recognize and call you father, as you know." But he did not go into the vineyard. And the father said to the second son, "Go and work in my vineyard." And the son said, "I will not. I do not acknowledge your authority. I do not see why I should obey you." But he went. And Jesus said, "Which of the two did the will of his father?" And those who heard him were in no doubt as to the answer. In one sense that is an over-simplification. But in another sense it offers to us a way of approach to this all-embracing problem of remaining faithful to the truth as we see it and at the same time maintaining that fervour and uniqueness which we attach to our Lord.

Because it is a practical issue, I want finally to say a word about the descriptive and definitive word which, in our preaching of tomorrow, will be absolutely vital and completely decisive. It is the word LOVE. If we are to preach in the days that lie ahead with the kind of acceptance with which our fathers were received, and with the kind of relevance which is demanded of us now, if we are to preach in such a way as to commend Jesus Christ, there is one complete and final expression of the meaning of reality. It is found in the suffering love of Christ. It is the modern translation of the words of Paul: "I am re-

solved to know nothing save Christ and Him crucified."
Here is the exposition of love. There are cheap and
sentimental ways in which love is offered by cheap-jacks
of one kind and another, which makes the true interpretation of love the more difficult for many people to appreci-
ate. If there is one overwhelming responsibility which
rests upon the Christian Church, and if there is one overwhelming responsibility which rests upon the hearts and
minds of preachers, it is to evaluate the concept of true
Christian love, which, as Bertrand Russell suggests, is the
only solvent of our needs.

Love, then, is not a sentiment, though it includes one.
It is not a feeling, though it includes feeling. The love of
Christ was goodwill on fire, indefatigable, undefeated.
The lack of that kind of goodwill in our public affairs
today is destroying the possibility of establishing world
government, the commonwealth of the people, that one
community of which Jesus speaks in the Sermon on the
Mount. Love is an unself-regarding, unselfish, persistent
goodwill which stops at nothing. It is not dependent on
the feelings that accompany it. It is an activity of the
personality which has its own rewards, but the exercise of
which is principally concerned in realizing the wages not
of comfort but of going on. Such goodwill is spoken
about almost every Sunday in every pulpit. But it is seen
uniquely in Jesus. The Jesus who cared for others,
who did them good, whether they cared about him or
not.

I am responsible for a hostel in London to which come
the poor relations of the down-and-outs, and utterly

destitute. About one hundred of these poor people are cared for. When we speak of this work to others, sometimes with a financial hope in mind, they often say to us, "Musn't it be lovely to care for these dear old people, to see how they respond to the kindness you bring to them, to watch their faces light up with gratitude and to comfort their last years with a sense of well being." And, of course, it isn't like that at all. They're not nice old people. They smell. Their habits are disagreeable. I don't blame them and neither must you. But the facts are that to surround them with a penumbra of sentimentality is to make a fundamental mistake. They are people you can't like. But you can love them, because love is an effective giving of one's self whether the elements of liking are present or not.

I'm very glad that I'm not asked to like people in the name of the Lord, because there are quite a lot of people I don't like, and they don't like me, and that's that. But you can love people. And that is the love of Jesus. During the war there was an efflorescence of voluntary service. It has decayed and disappeared until today you go far to find anybody who voluntarily expresses practical goodwill to his fellows. To preach that is not only in our day to meet a clamant need. It is in the days that lie ahead to meet an imperative one.

The second quality of love is tenderness. If we were suddenly startled into definition of tenderness, most of us would say that tenderness is an attitude of kindliness towards others. It's nothing of the sort. Intrinsically it's very different. Before I travelled to America I was compelled to be inoculated and vaccinated, and penetrated in one way and another, and for some time I had an arm rather like a balloon. During the time when it was like a balloon, of the eight million people living in London, about seven million seemed to bump into it. I am an expert on what tenderness is. Tenderness is the capacity to be hurt. That is Christian love—the capacity to be hurt —the refusal to put the cellophane of indifference around you. If somebody were to come up to me now and say to me, "Your little girl is seriously ill," that news would go through me like a knife. There are millions of little girls and boys in this world at the moment who are seriously ill. Does that go through me like a knife? Of course it doesn't. But it did go through the heart of Jesus like a knife. And that is tenderness. It is the yearning over those who are lost. It is the feeling of desolation for those who are perishing. It is the overwhelming sense that we have no right to enjoy the things which God has given to us unless we are tender and receptive; unless we concern ourselves by His grace with those who are dispossessed and outcast, the refugee, the prisoner, and those behind barbed wire.

This again is admittedly an emotional appeal and yet it lies at the heart of the kind of preaching which is desperately needed. Otherwise the Christian Church becomes an institution for caring for certain propositions, indulging in certain lucubrations, and, in fact, becoming irrelevant in communities where the principal and over-all responsibility is that men and women and little children may have enough to eat, and time to say their prayers, and nothing much to be afraid of if they hear a bang in the night. That is love. It is the love of Christ. When we say He bore our sorrows on the tree, what we mean is that though our area of love is so restrictive and only affects us, while our tenderness only extends to a small group, for Him the cry of the remotest child pierces His heart. I am not worthy to say these things, but they are true. And they are what we must preach about.

Above all, Jesus said that love is the taking up of a cross. A lady in my congregation said to me the other day that her cross was lumbago. Now I've had lumbago and I'm not inclined to smile at it as easily as some people do, but this degradation of the word is one from which it should be rescued. What did it mean for those who heard Jesus say, *take up a cross*? Something quite simple. Something quite unmistakable. Across the valley from where Jesus lived in Nazareth as a boy was the companion town of Sepphoris. We know what happened in Sepphoris. Judus, the Gaulonite, started a revolution or a resistance movement against the Roman Empire when Jesus was about eight years old, and Sepphoris was the seat of the insurrection. One bright morning the young men of Sepphoris threw out the little Roman garrison with their own improvised weapons. They set up the banners of independence and they proclaimed themselves free. And Jesus must have seen it. But the Romans were a thorough-going people and they came back. They came back with a large army and they bashed in the puny defences of Sepphoris. With their usual thoroughness, having overcome the young men, they burnt Sepphoris to the ground. They took away the women into honourable or dishonourable captivity. They killed off most of the old people. Then, as was their custom, they crucified the young men who remained, and Jesus must have seen those crosses against the sky. Every young man who was crucified knew that part of the penalty which ended in agonizing death was that when he was sentenced he had to take up the piece of wood upon which he was to suffer, and he had to carry it to the place where he was to die.

The man who took up his cross was the man who was performing the last free act of his life. He was, in very truth, looking death in the face. There was nothing more that could be required of a man after he had carried his cross because that was the last free action of his body. And those who listened to Jesus speak of taking up a cross had that sense of the ultimate, that sense of inevitability, that sense of finality. That is the ultimate concept of love. It is going on to the end. And if there is any beyond, it is offering to go there, too.

If the essence of our preaching lies in bringing the world to see the redeeming love of Christ, then we shall best advocate Him as we declare His love. For it is still true:

See, from His head, His hands, His feet,
Sorrow and love flow mingled down:
Did e'er such love and sorrow meet,
Or thorns compose so rich a crown?

Were the whole realm of nature mine,
That were an offering far too small;
Love so amazing, so divine,
Demands my soul, my life, my all.